THE ✦ SCOTTISH
COOK BOOK

Originally published in 1921
First published 2014

Amberley Publishing
The Hill, Stroud
Gloucestershire, GL5 4EP

www.amberley-books.com

British Library Cataloguing in Publication Data.
A catalogue record for this book is available from the British Library.

ISBN 978 1 4456 4338 0 (print)
ISBN 978 1 4456 4346 5 (ebook)

Typeset in 10pt on 12pt Sabon.
Typesetting and Origination by Amberley Publishing.
Printed in the UK.

Contents

This and previous page: Courtesy of the Library of Congress.

Introduction

Scotland, with its temperate climate and abundance of game, has provided a cornucopia of food for its inhabitants for millennia. The wealth of seafood available on and off the coasts provided sustenance for the earliest settlers. Agriculture was introduced, with primitive oats quickly becoming the staple. During the nineteenth and twentieth centuries there was large-scale immigration to Scotland from Italy, and later from the Middle East, Pakistan and India. These cultures have influenced Scots cooking dramatically.

Mrs Alan Breck, a cookery consultant of unuusual talent and experience, who studied her craft under many conditions and in several countries at the start of the twentieth century, laid down much of her practical knowledge in the original edition of this book, 'The Mrs Alan Breck Recipe Book'. In this, the quintessential Scottish cook book, the history of Scottish cuisine is explored, with traditional recipes such as Haggis, Kedgeree, Aberdeen Haddock, Mulligatawny Soup, Eggs Fried in Batter, and Dundee Cake. It is not intended as a total guide to Scottish cuisine - there are no deep-fried Mars bars here - but rather a window into its development at the turn of the century. There are also numerous household and economical tips from from a master of the trade.

In the following Recipes a spoonful of dry ingredients means as much above as in the bowl of the spoon. Half a spoonful means what remains in the spoon after the back of a knife has been drawn across it. A liquid spoonful is always level with the edge of the spoon.

SOUPS.

STOCK SEASONINGS. (1)

Many people have rather vague ideas of the proportion of vegetables, etc., generally used in making stock. It is a mistake to use a quantity of one vegetable because it happens to be convenient and to omit others, if a well balanced flavour is wanted.

The following quantities will be found sufficient for each quart of Stock :—

1 tablespoonful Carrot.
1 tablespoonful Turnip.
½ tablespoonful Parsnip.
½ teaspoonful Salt.
¼ teaspoonful Celery Seed or
   ½ tablespoonful Celery Root
2 Cloves.

1 Onion.
3 Peppercorns.
2 Allspice Berries.
½ teaspoonful Mixed Herbs.
½ a Bay Leaf.
1 sprig Parsley.

The celery seed and herbs should be tied in a muslin, and the cloves stuck in the onion.

AMERICAN PEA SOUP. (2)

½ lb. Split Peas.	1 large Onion
½ lb. Neck of Mutton.	2 ozs. Carrot.
½ pint Tomato Purée.	2 ozs Turnip.
¼ teaspoonful Sugar.	3 pints Cold Water.
10 White Peppercorns.	Salt.

Wash carefully and soak the peas overnight. Wipe and cut the mutton up small and put it on in the water with the peas and bring to the boil. Skim and add the remaining ingredients except the tomatoes and salt. Let all boil gently for 2½ hours then add the tomatoes and boil another ½ hour. Pass through a fine sieve, re-heat, add salt and serve hot.

JERUSALEM ARTICHOKE SOUP. (3)

2 lbs. Artichokes	2 pints White Stock.
1 Onion.	1 pint Milk.
1½ ozs. Butter.	Salt and Pepper.
1 oz. Cornflour.	Lemon Juice or Vinegar.
2 sticks Celery.	

Wash the artichokes and peel them thinly keeping them under water as much as possible to prevent them getting black. As they are peeled drop them into cold water to which some lemon juice or a few drops of vinegar have been added. Prepare the onion and celery and slice them. Drain and slice the artichokes and sauté them in the butter in a well lined pan but do not let them brown. Add the stock and let all simmer for an hour. Pass through a hair sieve, re-heat and add the cornflour broken in a little cold water. Let it boil 8 minutes then add the milk and re-heat but do not let it boil. Season very well and serve with fried dice of bread. A little cream is a great improvement to this soup.

ASPARAGUS SOUP.   (4)

1 tin Asparagus.	1½ ozs. Butter.
1 qt. White Stock.	2 ozs. Flour.
1 Rasher of Bacon.	1 small Onion.
Sprig of Parsley.	8 White Peppercorns.
1 Pint Milk.	Salt.

Open a tin of asparagus, drain off the liquor and rinse in cold water. Cut off the points with a sharp knife and lay aside. Cut the remainder of the asparagus in inch lengths.

Melt the butter in a lined pan, add the onion which should be scalded and cut in rings and fry but do not brown. Add the bacon cut into pieces and the asparagus and cook gently for 10 minutes, then add the flour and mix well. Thin down with the stock, add seasonings and when it comes to the boil skim it.   Let it simmer for ¾ of an hour then pass through a hair sieve and rub through as much of the asparagus pulp as possible. Bring to the boil and add the asparagus points. Heat the milk separately and add the soup to it in the tureen. Season and serve very hot.

AUCKLAND TOMATO SOUP.   (5)

1 oz. Butter.	1 large Onion.
1½ ozs. Flour.	2 large Carrots.
1 Blade Mace.	6 large Tomatoes.
1 teaspoonful Sugar.	6 Cloves.
1 quart Water.	6 White Peppercorns.
4 tablespoonsful Cream.	Salt.

Slice onion, grate one of the carrots and fry these in the butter.   Add the sugar and tomatoes sliced and fry these also.   Add the water, put lid on saucepan and let it come slowly to the boil.   Slice the second carrot and add it with the spices and let all simmer for 1½ hours.   Add the flour broken perfectly smoothly with a little cold water and boil 15 minutes longer. Pass through a fine sieve, re-heat, season and add the cream, which must not be allowed to boil in the soup.

BROWN VEGETABLE SOUP. (6)

2 Carrots.	2 Potatoes.
½ Swedish Turnip.	1 tablespoonful Chopped Parsley.
1 Onion.	3 tablespoonsful Flour.
2 Leeks.	1½ tablespoonsful Dripping.
3 pints Cold Water.	Salt and Pepper.

Clean the vegetables and cut up in small dice. Make the dripping hot in a soup pot and when blue smoke rises from it fry all the vegetables, except the leeks and parsley, till brown. Add the flour and brown it also. Then add the water by degrees, stirring vigorously to prevent lumps. When it boils add the leeks and seasonings. Let it boil 2 to 2½ hours and before serving add the chopped parsley. If liked, one of the carrots can be grated and added with the leek.

CARROT SOUP. (7)

2 lbs. Carrots.	1½ tablespoonsful fine Sago
1 oz. Ham or Bacon.	1 large Onion.
½ oz. Margarine.	2 sticks Celery or
½ pint Milk.	¼ teaspoonful Celery Seed.
1 tablespoonful Chopped	3 pints Stock.
Parsley.	Salt and Pepper.

Choose as red carrots as possible ; wash, scrape and grate half of them and cut the others in slices. Scald and slice the onion thinly. Clean and cut up the celery. Melt the margarine in a pan and add the bacon cut up. Add the prepared vegetables to it and put on a lid and let it cook gently for 15 minutes without browning. Add the stock and let all come to the boil. Skim well and add the sago. Let all cook gently for 1½ hours then pass through a hair or very fine wire sieve.

Reheat the soup, season well and add the chopped parsley. Heat the milk separately and add to the soup in the tureen. Serve with fried dice of bread.

CHESTNUT SOUP.   (8)

1 lb. Chestnuts.	2 Onions.
2½ pints White Stock.	1 Stick Celery.
½ pint Milk.	6 White Peppercorns.
1½ ozs. Butter.	1 oz. Flour.
Salt.	Carmine.

Slit each chestnut and put on in cold water to boil. Boil for 15 minutes, remove skins and peel them. Melt the butter in a pan and add the onions in slices and celery in short pieces. Let them cook till nicely browned in the butter. Add the flour and then thin down with the stock, then add the chestnuts and seasonings and simmer for one hour. Pass through a very fine sieve and mix quite smooth. Return to pan, add the milk, reheat to boiling point and season very well. If the colour is not good add a few drops of carmine to improve it. Needless to say this should be very cautiously done.

Chestnuts vary a good deal in flouriness and sometimes quite a number out of a pound are not good, so the thickness of the soup must be left to the judgment of the cook, who can add or leave out some milk or stock if necessary.

The flavour is best when the onions are cooked slowly in the butter and not hurriedly browned.

An old saucepan should be used for boiling the chestnuts before the skin is removed.

SUPERIOR COCK-A-LEEKIE.   (9)

1 Fowl.	1 lb. Shin of Beef.
1 doz. Leeks.	3 quarts Water.
1 doz. Prunes.	Salt and Pepper.

Wash and soak the prunes. Wash the leeks very thoroughly. Wipe the beef and remove marrow from the bone ; put it on with the 3 quarts cold water and when it comes to the boil skim carefully. Let it boil gently for one hour, then add the fowl trussed for boiling and 2 leeks cut up rather finely, using only the white part. Add salt and let soup simmer another hour then add the prunes and the remaining leeks cut in two lengthwise and then in half-inch pieces, using about one inch of the green part. Boil gently for another hour. When the fowl has been boiling for an hour and a half take it out and cut up the best parts into neat pieces and return to the soup. Reheat, remove the shin of beef and season well. Serve very hot.

CURRIED POTATO SOUP.   (10)

1½ lbs. Potatoes.	½ Apple.
2 Onions.	1½ teaspoonsful Curry Powder.
1 oz. Margarine.	1 quart Stock.
1 gill Milk.	½ teaspoonful Vinegar.
¼ teaspoonful Celery Seed.	Salt.

Peel and slice thinly the vegetables and apple and fry in the margarine. Add the curry powder and fry for 5 minutes, being careful that the potato does not stick or brown. Add the stock when it boils, the salt, and the celery seed tied in a scrap of muslin. Add the vinegar and simmer for 1½ hours. Pass through a sieve, add the milk and re-heat. A squeeze of lemon may be added at the last moment.

Water in which meat, beans or lentils have been boiled may be substituted for stock and half a stick of rhubarb may be added in place of apple, if more convenient.

FRENCH VEGETABLE SOUP.　(11)

This is one of the most delicious vegetable soups which is made without stock and, if carefully prepared, it is quite worthy to take its place with much more pretentious soups.

2 Potatoes.	¼ cup Turnip.
2 Tomatoes.	2 Sticks Celery.
1 Carrot.	2 Onions.
1½ ozs. Seed Tapioca.	1 tablespoonful Chopped Parsley.
1 oz. Butter.	½ teaspoonful Sugar,
3 pints Water.	¼ pint Milk.
Pepper and Salt.	¼ pint Cream.

Wash and peel the vegetables except the parsley ; cut up in rough dice. Heat the butter in a pan, add the vegetables and sugar and cook for 8 to 10 minutes but do not let them brown. Add cold water and bring to the boil. Add the tapioca and boil gently for 1½ hours. Pass through a hair sieve and add the parsley very finely chopped. Re-heat and season well. Heat the milk and cream to almost boiling point and pour into the tureen. Add the soup to this, stirring all the time. Serve with cheese fingers.

ILLYRIAN SOUP. (12)

Is always much appreciated if made with a good white stock not too strongly flavoured.

2 slices Bacon.	2 Potatoes.
3 Carrots.	Small piece of Turnip.
2 Onions.	1 quart White Stock.
½ oz. Sago.	2 tablespoonsful of Cream.
Walnut of Butter.	½ teaspoonful Sugar.
Salt and Pepper.	

Put the bacon at the bottom of a lined stew pan, add the vegetables cut small, the sugar and the stock. Bring to the boil and add the sago. Simmer very gently till the vegetables are quite soft, about 2½ hours. Rub through a hair sieve, re-heat and season. Heat the cream and butter in a small pan and pour into a tureen to which add the soup, stirring all the time. Serve with cheese fingers.

JUGGED SOUP. (13)

This is a most delicious soup if made with delicately flavoured stock. The liquid in which fresh beef or mutton has been boiled is very suitable.

1 gill Potatoes.	1 gill Tomato Pulp.
½ gill Carrot.	1 gill Shelled Peas.
½ gill Turnip.	2 tablespoonsful Rice.
½ gill Onion.	3 pints Stock.
Salt and Pepper.	Pinch of Jamaica Pepper.

Cut potatoes, carrot, turnip and onion into small dice and put in layers in a stone jar. Add the peas and washed rice then tomato, salt and peppers. Pour over all the stock. Cover with a greased paper and then a lid and cook steadily in the oven for 3 hours.

If more convenient, put jar in pan with water half way up and steam same length of time.

LEWIS SOUP. (14)

1 lb. Haddock.	1 Onion.
1 Carrot.	$\frac{1}{2}$ blade Mace
Small Piece Turnip.	4 Cloves.
1 dozen Peppercorns.	1 oz. Butter.
$\frac{1}{2}$ dozen sprigs Parsley.	4 pints Water.
3 ozs. Rice.	1 tablespoonful Chopped Parsley
Salt.	2 dessertspoonsful Concentrated
2 sticks Celery.	Tomato Purée.

Well wash and fillet the haddock. Melt the butter in a pan and sweat the cut up onion, celery and turnip in it. Add the cold water and the fish with bones, head, etc. When it boils skim and add the carrot grated and the parsley and seasonings. Cook gently for an hour and a quarter and pass through a sieve. Return the soup to the rinsed pan, add the tomato purée and when it boils add the rice which should be well washed, and boil for 25 minutes. Five minutes before serving add the chopped parsley and a few flakes of the fish and serve very hot and well seasoned.

If liked a teacupful of sieved tinned tomato can be used in place of the concentrated purée.

MULLIGATAWNY SOUP (PLAIN). (15)

Bones. etc., of 2 Rabbits.	Small piece Turnip.
1 large Onion.	Small piece Carrot.
1 large Apple.	1 dessertspoonful Curry Powder.
1$\frac{1}{2}$ ozs. Flour.	2 pints 2nd Stock.
2 ozs. Bacon Fat.	1 pint Water.
Salt and Lemon Juice.	

When a galantine of rabbit has been made this soup will be found useful for using up the bones, etc.

B

Wash and cleanse the rabbits and remove the meat required for the galantine then cut up in neat pieces. Skin the onion and cut in slices and peel and chop the apple. Fry the rabbit in the bacon fat then the onion apple curry powder and flour. When nicely browned add the stock by degrees and let it come to the boil. Skim and add the prepared vegetables and the salt. Let all simmer two hours and strain through a fine sieve.

Re-heat and season, and last of all add lemon juice to taste. Serve with well-boiled rice handed separately.

PURÉE OF ONIONS. (16)

2 doz. small Garden Onions or Syboes.	12 White Pepper Corns.
	½ pint Milk.
2 ozs. Butter.	2 ozs. Flour.
2½ pints Light Stock.	Salt.

Wash and slice the onions and fry in 1 oz. butter but do not let them brown. When the butter is absorbed add the stock, pepper corns and salt and simmer for 1½ hours. Pass through a hair sieve.

Melt the remainder of the butter in a pan and add the flour and cook for a few seconds. Thin down gradually with the soup, beating any lumps out before it gets thin, stir till it boils and cook for 15 minutes. Add the milk, season more if necessary, bring to boiling point and serve at once with fried dice of bread handed separately.

PUMPKIN SOUP. (17)

2 lbs. Prepared Pumpkin.	2 ozs. Flour.
2 Onions.	1 teaspoonful Sugar.
2 ozs. Butter.	2 pints Water.
6 White Peppercorns.	$\frac{1}{2}$ pint Milk.
Salt.	Grated Cheese or Diced Toast.

Prepare the pumpkin by removing the skin, seeds and fluffy part from the centre and cut in small pieces. Slice the onions and fry in the butter, then add pumpkin and mix well. Put on lid and let all cook gently for half an hour but do not let it brown. Add the sugar, peppercorns and salt with the water and boil up. Skim well and simmer for an hour and a half, then pass through a fine sieve and re-heat. Mix the flour smoothly with a little water and add to the soup. Let it cook another 10 minutes. Bring the milk to the boil and pour into tureen then add the soup to this. Season and serve with grated cheese or small dice of toast handed separately.

VEGETABLE MARROW SOUP. (18)

2 lbs. Vegetable Marrow.	2 pints White Stock.
2 Onions.	2 ozs. Butter.
2 gills Milk.	1 oz. Cornflour.
$\frac{1}{4}$ teaspoonful Celery Seed.	Salt and Pepper.

Peel marrow, remove seeds and cut in pieces. Peel and slice onions and fry these vegetables in the butter, but do not brown them. After 5 minutes add the stock and when it boils add celery seed tied in a scrap of muslin. Simmer $1\frac{1}{2}$ hours and pass through hair sieve. Re-heat and when it boils add the cornflour broken in the milk. Stir till it boils and let it cook 7 minutes.

Water may be substituted for stock but grated cheese should be handed with the soup if this is done.

VEGETARIAN CLEAR SOUP.   (19)

This is a very good soup and with a fairly substantial dish to follow, it will be found a valuable addition to the menu of housewives who have to study economy closely.

1 lb. Carrots.	2 small Onions.
1 lb. Turnip.	3 teaspoonsful Marmite Veget-
12 Black Peppercorns.	able Extract.
2 lumps Sugar.	Salt.
2 quarts Water.	½ glass Sherry
3 Portugal Onions.	

Scrape the carrots, peel the turnip and cut in slices. Peel the onions and cut up roughly. Put these into a soup pan with the cold water, salt and peppercorns. Let all come slowly to the boil and boil gently for 4 to 5 hours. Pass through a straining cloth or hair sieve. Rinse the pan, re-heat the stock and add the marmite and sugar, then bring to boiling point. The sherry should now be added but it is by no means necessary. Serve the soup very hot and hand cheese fingers with it.

If liked, some julienne strips of carrot may be added as a garnish.

FISH.

ABERDEEN HADDOCK AND TOMATO. (20)

2 Aberdeen Haddocks.	3 large Tomatoes.
1 Onion.	1 oz. Butter.
Breadcrumbs.	1 Dessertspoonful Parsley.
Pepper.	Margarine.

Lay the haddocks on a flat dish and cover with boiling water. After 3 minutes remove the skins and cut each in four. Skin the tomatoes; skin, scald, and slice the onion thinly and chop the parsley. Fry the onion a pale brown in the butter then add the tomatoes cut in slices. Put on a lid and cook gently till tender.

Lay the haddocks on a greased fireproof dish and cover with the onion and tomato mixture. Sprinkle the chopped parsley over and season to taste. Cover with a layer of fresh breadcrumbs and dot a few pieces of margarine over. Bake for half an hour in a moderate oven and serve hot.

COD'S ROE WITH BACON. (21)

1 Cod's Roe.	Vinegar.
½ lb. Bacon.	Flour.
Salt.	Pepper.

Wash the roe but do not let it lie in water. If the skin is broken tie roe in muslin and put into salted boiling water to which a few drops of vinegar have been added. Let it simmer gently from 25 to 30 minutes according to thickness. Drain and cool and cut into slices about half an inch thick.

Fry the bacon lightly and keep warm over hot water. Pass the slices of roe through some seasoned flour and fry in the bacon fat. Serve on a hot dish with the bacon round.

SALT COD AND PARSNIP PURÉE.   (22)

1 lb. Salt Cod.	Parsnip Purée.
½ pint Egg Sauce.	Chopped Parsley.

Procure a carton of boneless and skinless salt cod as it is quite the nicest salt fish and there is no waste.

Wash well and let it soak in tepid water for 12 hours changing the water three times.

Put it on with cold water and bring slowly to the boil and at once pour off all the water and cover with boiling water or, better still, half water and half milk. Cook it very gently so that it doesn't boil for about half an hour when it should be tender. With two forks break it into flakes and mix with the egg sauce which should not be at all thin.

Have a hot dish with a border of parsnip purée arranged on it and into the centre pile up the fish and sprinkle with finely chopped parsley.

N.B.—Always use two forks or a silver knife and fork in flaking the cod as it is very sensitive to the action of steel.

FISH SOUFFLÉ.   (23)

1 breakfastcup Cooked Chopped Fish.	2 teaspoonsful Chopped Parsley.
1 teacup Cooked Potato.	2 tablespoonsful Milk or Cream.
2 rounded tablespoonsful Butter.	2 raw Eggs.
	Salt and Pepper.

Butter a deep soufflé or pie dish. Melt butter, add the potato mashed and beat together till hot and light. Add the prepared fish, parsley, milk, yolks of eggs and seasonings, and lastly the stiffly beaten whites of eggs. Place in dish and cook at once in a hot oven till brown and puffed up. Serve at once in the dish it has been cooked in.

HADDOCKS WHITEBAIT FASHION.   (24)

2 Haddocks (1 lb. each).	1 Lemon.
Flour.	Salt and Pepper.
Brown Bread and Butter.	Parsley.

Fillet the haddocks and see that the side bones are removed. Cut up in pieces about 2 inches long and $\frac{1}{2}$ an inch wide and toss in flour seasoned with salt and pepper. Lay on a sieve and shake well to separate each piece and remove superfluous flour. Put in a frying basket and fry in deep fat till golden brown. Drain well on kitchen paper and dish in a heap on a folded napkin. Garnish with lemon and parsley. Hand thin slices of bread and butter with the fish. Plaice is very nice done in this way.

MAYONNAISE OF HALIBUT.   (25)

Place a steak of halibut on a greased baking dish and season with salt, pepper and a squeeze of lemon juice. Cover with a greased paper and bake in a moderate oven for 20 minutes.

Remove the skin when cold, lay on a entrée dish on a bed of fresh lettuce leaves. Coat with mayonnaise and make a neat decoration with tiny rounds of fresh tomato and capers cut in halves.

BAKED HERRINGS HOLLANDAISE.   (26)

In this country the homely but excellent herring is seldom seen except at the breakfast table, but prepared in the following way it is quite worthy of a place on the dinner menu where it makes a pleasant variety.

4 Herrings.	Lemon Juice.
1 oz. Flour.	½ pint Fish Stock.
1 oz. Butter.	1 teaspoonful Vinegar.
1 teaspoonful Capers.	1 teaspoonful Made Mustard.
Salt and Pepper.	

Fillet the herrings, removing all bones.   Rub well with salt and pepper and lay in a cool place for at least an hour. Lay on a greased baking dish, add a dash of lemon juice to each fillet, cover with a greased paper and bake in a good oven for 10 minutes.   Serve with the following sauce handed separately.

Melt butter in saucepan, add flour and blend thoroughly. Add gradually the fish stock and beat well to free from lumps.   Let it boil gently for 10 minutes, then add the mustard, vinegar, capers and seasoning of salt and pepper.

GRILLED RED HERRINGS.   (27)

An extremely inexpensive but savoury dish can be prepared for the breakfast table from the simple red herring.   If cooked in this way it will be found very palatable indeed.

Soak as many red herrings as you require in plenty of cold water for 24 hours.   Change the water twice during that time.   Split the herrings open and rinse in fresh water.   Wipe and grill them for eight minutes under the gas or in front of a clear fire.   Serve very hot with a pat of fresh butter and squeeze of lemon juice on each.

ECONOMICAL KEDGEREE. (28)

½ lb. Cooked Kippered Herring.	1 Cook's Egg.
¼ lb. Rice.	2 ozs. Margarine.
Salt and Pepper.	Pinch of Nutmeg.

Free the kippers from skin and bone then weigh. Boil the rice till tender and drain well.

Melt the margarine in a stew pan, add the fish and rice and mix very well. Make thoroughly hot and add the Cook's egg beaten lightly. Last of all add the seasonings. Mix and pile on a hot dish and garnish with slices of lemon and parsley.

STEAMED KIPPERS. (29)

Those who find kippers too heavy and greasy should try this method of cooking them.

Lay the kippers skin up upon a deep plate and pour boiling water on them. After 5 minutes drain them and steam them between two plates for an hour with a dust of pepper and a tiny pat of butter to each.

FILLETS OF MACKEREL. (30)

3 Mackerel.	Salt and Pepper.
1 oz. Margarine.	Parsley.

Skin and fillet the mackerel which should be very fresh. Rub the fillets with salt and pepper and roll with the side which was next the bone out. Lay on a greased baking sheet, cover with greased paper and bake in a moderate oven for 15 minutes. Dish up in a circle and pour gooseberry sauce over and round. Garnish with parsley.

NORWEGIAN FISH PIE. (31)

1 lb. Filleted Haddock.	1 oz. Flour.
1 gill Milk.	1 oz. Butter.
2 Eggs.	¼ teaspoonful Made Mustard.
Salt and Pepper.	Lemon Juice.

Steam the haddock between two greased plates then flake it up rather finely with a silver knife and fork.

Melt the butter in a saucepan and add the flour then the gill of milk which may be made up with the juice which runs from the fish in cooking. Beat till quite smooth then let it cook for 5 minutes. Let it cool a little and add the yolks of the eggs and beat them in very thoroughly. Add the flaked fish, mustard, salt and pepper and a good dash of lemon juice. Lastly fold in the whites of eggs very stiffly beaten. Bake in a very well greased soufflé or pie dish for half an hour and serve at once after taking from the oven.

Hand cut lemon with the pie.

PLAICE À L'ORLY. (32)

1 Plaice filleted.	Frying Batter.
Marinade :—1 tablespoonful Salad Oil.	1 teaspoonful Chopped Parsley.
Juice of ½ a Lemon.	½ teaspoonful Chopped Shallot.
Salt and Pepper.	Pinch of Cayenne.

Cut the fillets into neat pieces diagonally and lay in the marinade for an hour, turning them after the first half-hour. Dip in the batter and fry a golden brown. Garnish with lemon and fried parsley and serve with tomato sauce handed separately.

Frying Batter :—

2 ozs. Flour.	2 tablespoonsful Milk.
1 whole Egg and 1 Yolk.	Salt and Pepper.
1 tablespoonful Salad Oil.	

Make the batter at least an hour before it is wanted as it improves with standing.

Sieve flour and salt into a basin, add yolks of eggs and milk and beat till quite smooth. Gradually work in the oil. Just before it is to be used add the white of egg very stiffly beaten.

STUFFED PLAICE. (33)

2 Plaice.	1 teaspoonful Breadcrumbs.
4 Sardines.	½ teaspoonful Lemon Juice.
Pepper and Salt.	½ pint Parsley Sauce.
1 teaspoonful Chopped Parsley.	

Bone sardines and free them from skin and oil. Pound with the breadcrumbs, parsley and seasonings. Fillet the plaice and spread each fillet with the mixture. Roll up and tie with strong sewing cotton. Lay on a greased baking tin, cover with greased paper and bake for 15 minutes. Remove cotton, dish up and pour sauce round.

BAKED SALMON. (34)

3 small Steaks of Chilled Salmon.	6 Black Pepper Corns.
	1 teacup Water.
1 teacup Vinegar.	½ teaspoonful Salt.

Let the salmon lie in the warm kitchen till it is quite thawed. Rinse it in cold water and lay in a pie dish so that the steaks slightly overlap one another. Mix the other ingredients together and pour over the fish. Bake in a moderate oven for ¾ of an hour and serve cold.

GATEAU DE SAUMON.   (35)

¾ lb. Cooked Salmon.	¾ gill Milk.
½ teacupful Bread Crumbs.	2 Eggs.
1 oz. Butter. Salt.	¼ teaspoonful Pepper.

Break up the fish with a silver knife and fork and remove bones.   Mix it well with the dry ingredients.   Heat the milk slightly and melt the butter in it.   Add it to the yolks of eggs well beaten and mix with the fish.   Last of all fold in the stiffly beaten whites of eggs.   Turn into a well greased mould and steam for one hour.

Dish carefully and coat with ½ pint well made parsley sauce and hand cut lemon separately.

SCALLOPED FISH À LA MORNY.   (36)

½ oz. Butter	2 ozs. Cheese.
½ oz. Flour.	6 ozs. Cooked Fish.
½ pint Milk.	Salt and Pepper.

Butter some shells and lay aside.   Melt the butter in a saucepan, add the flour, mix well and by degrees add the milk, beating well to make the sauce smooth and glossy. Grate the cheese and add two-thirds of it to the sauce. Flake the fish, add to the sauce and season well.   Heap up in the shells and dust the remainder of the grated cheese on top and brown in a good oven.   The cheese should be Parmesan.

FILETS DE SOLES DANOISE.   (37)

This makes an exceedingly pretty dish if it is daintily prepared.

2 Soles.	Lemon Juice.
½ oz. Butter.	½ gill White Wine.
Salt and Pepper.	Brown Bread Crumbs.

Sauce :—

1 oz. Butter.	½ oz. Parmesan Cheese.
½ oz. Flour.	½ gill Fish Stock.
1 dessertspoonful Anchovy	½ gill Milk.
Essence.	Pepper.

Garnish :—

1 oz. Butter.	Lemon Juice.
1 tablespoonful Chopped	Parsley.
Parsley.	

Fillet the soles season with salt and pepper and roll round the little finger. Place on a greased baking dish and add a dash of lemon juice to each. Pour the wine round, cover with a greased paper and poach in the oven for 15 minutes.

Have the crumbs a golden brown and passed through a fine sieve. Heat these and roll the fillets in them as soon as they come out of the oven, otherwise they won't stick. Shake off superfluous crumbs and lay on a hot entrée dish and pour the sauce round. Garnish with roses of Maître d'hôtel butter just before sending to table.

To prepare the sauce, melt butter in pan, add flour, and mix, but do not brown. Thin down with the fish stock and then the milk. Let it cook 10 minutes and add the cheese and anchovy essence and season.

To prepare the garnish chop the parsley very finely, mix with the butter and lemon juice. Put into a forcing bag, with a medium sized rose, and pipe on to a flat dish. Stick a tiny sprig of very stiff parsley into the middle of each rose and set on ice or in a very cold place till quite hard.

SOLES FARCES À LA MAYONNAISE. (38)

2 small Soles.	3 gills Aspic Jelly.
1 gill Picked Shrimps.	½ gill Cream.
1 gill Mayonnaise.	Salt and Pepper.
Lemon Juice.	White Sauce.
¼ oz. Gelatine.	Lettuce and Cooked Carrot.

Pound the shrimps with about 2 tablespoonsful of white sauce till a nice paste is formed. Fillet the soles and lay with skin sides uppermost. Season with salt, pepper and lemon juice. Spread with the shrimp mixture which should be well seasoned. Fold in two and lay on a well greased baking sheet, cover with greased paper and bake for 15 minutes. Dissolve 1 gill of the aspic and melt the gelatine in it. Let it cool and strain it into the mayonnaise then add the cream lightly whipped. When the soles are cold coat them with the aspic mayonnaise and let them set. Coat again and garnish with very tiny rounds of the reddest part of the carrot. Coat each with a spoonful of half-set aspic and dress, when set, on a bed of lettuce. Chop the remainder of the aspic jelly and garnish the dish with tiny heaps of it.

WHITING À LA PARISIENNE. (39)

6 Whiting.	1 dessertspoonful Chopped
Lemon Juice.	Parsley.

Salt and Pepper.

Have the whiting skinned but not turned. Lay them on a buttered fireproof dish and dust with salt and pepper ; add a squeeze of lemon juice to each and sprinkle with parsley. Cover closely with a well buttered paper and bake 15 minutes in a good oven. Serve with brown bread and butter.

MEAT.

AMERICAN STEAK.

This steak is one of the most savoury dishes one could imagine and is always much appreciated if the directions are carefully carried out.

1½ lb. Steak (2 in. thick).	Flour and Margarine.
2 large Onions.	Pepper and Salt.
½ lb. Tomatoes.	

Lay the steak on a thickly floured board and dredge more flour on top of it. With the edge of a strong kitchen plate beat the steak for 5 minutes, always keeping it well floured. When half beaten turn the steak round so that it is beaten both up and down and across. Turn the steak right over and if necessary add more flour and beat underside also for 5 minutes.

Heat some margarine in a frying pan and fry the onion cut in small dice till it is golden brown, then add the tomatoes and fry also. The tomatoes should be peeled and cut in half. Put the steak into a stew pan and brown it on both sides, also any flour from the board. Add the salt and pepper, onion and tomato and 2 tablespoons of water. Put on the lid and let it simmer very gently for at least 3 hours. The chief points to remember are the thorough beating and flouring of the steak and the slow cooking.

BEEF STEAK À LA RUSSE. (41)

1 lb. Pope's Eye Steak.	Egg and Bread Crumbs.
3 ozs. Fresh Butter.	Salt and Pepper.
1 tablespoonful Chopped Parsley.	3 Bananas.

Mince the steak finely and mix it with the fresh butter, which should be creamed with the parsley and salt and pepper. Form into round cakes about ¾ of an inch thick. Dip in egg and breadcrumbs and fry in shallow fat till nicely browned on both sides. Both egg and breadcrumbs should be seasoned. Cut the bananas across in half and then in half lengthwise. Dip in egg and breadcrumbs and fry till brown. Dish the cakes on a border of mashed potato and fill the centre with the fried bananas. Pour half a pint of good brown sauce round and serve at once.

BAKED BEEF STEAK. (42)

1¼ lbs. Pope's Eye Steak.	Flour.
Salt and Pepper.	Maître d'hôtel Butter.

Have the steak cut 1½ to 2 inches thick. Put some salt and pepper into it on both sides, then flour it liberally with seasoned flour. Lay it into a perfectly dry casserole, put a piece of paper over the top of the casserole and then the lid.

Put into an oven hot enough to cook a roast and cook for two hours, turning the steak from time to time, but do not prick it with a fork as all the juice must be kept in.

When done lay on a hot dish and put the casserole on the stove. Add sufficient boiling water to make a nice gravy, mixing well with the flour, etc., which will be sticking to the dish. Season the gravy, boil up and pour round the steak. Just as it goes to table lay a few pats of Maître d'hôtel butter on top.

Serve with potato chips.

N.B.—A steak and an equal sized slice of leg of mutton cooked on top of one another in this way make a delightful combination.

BRAISED BEEF. (43)

2 Ribs of Beef.	1 oz. Butter.
2 ozs. Fat Bacon.	3 Onions.
½ Bay Leaf.	4 Cloves.
½ Blade Mace.	2 sticks Celery.
4 Sprigs Parsley.	3 pieces Turnip.
3 Carrots.	Salt.
1½ doz. Peppercorns.	

This method of cooking beef is not, accurately speaking, braising neither is it boiling but it is quite an excellent one. Get the ribs of beef boned and rolled. Put the bacon free from rind and rust in a dry deep soup pot to quite cover the bottom. Then add the butter and 2 of the onions sliced. Lay in the beef, put on the lid and let it cook over a good heat for 20 minutes. Turn the meat after 10 minutes being careful not to pierce it with a fork or the juice will escape. After 20 minutes fill up the pan with hot water to cover the meat, add the bones, vegetables and seasonings, sticking the cloves in the remaining onion. The vegetables should be cut in neat pieces suitable for a garnish but not too small. Let all come to the boil and

c

skim very well indeed then draw aside and let it cook very slowly for 4 hours. Watch it carefully so that it never boils and if necessary set the pan on a trivet to prevent this. It should cook just below boiling point.

Serve with the vegetables round and a good sauce made from some of the liquor.

Strain the liquor through a hair sieve or cloth and lay aside till next day. When the fat has been removed an excellent brown soup will be ready for use after re-heating. If the directions are carefully followed it will be found quite sufficiently clear and only a garnish need be added.

This meat is very good cold, having more flavour than roast beef. Silverside may be used in place of ribs.

BRAISED TONGUE.   (44)

Boil a fresh tongue gently for 2 hours with 2 carrots and a bunch of herbs in the water. Remove skin and roots. Put into a deep pot with a pint of hot sauce and 2 table-spoonsful each of carrot, onion, celery and tomato. Add ¼ of a blade of mace, 2 pimento berries and a sprig of parsley. Cover with a greased paper and braise slowly in the oven for 2 hours. Turn the tongue after 1 hour. Dish up and strain the sauce round. Garnish with mounds of boiled spinach.

Sauce :—

1½ ozs. Butter.	1 pint liquor from Tongue.
1½ ozs. Flour.	Seasonings.

Brown the butter and flour very slowly together and thin down with the liquor. Boil up and season well.

AN INVALID'S CHOP. (45)

Choose a chop from a well hung loin of home fed mutton. Cut away most of the fat and trim neatly.

Lay on a lightly buttered soup plate, add a pinch of salt and pepper, cover with a buttered paper and then a lid.

Place over a stew pan with plenty of fast boiling water and steam steadily for ¾ of an hour, turning the chop once during the time. Serve on a hot plate with any of the juice that has run from it poured over.

DUTCH ROLL WITH ORANGE SALAD. (46)

1 lb. Lean Mutton.	1 dessertspoonful Chutney.
2 tablespoonsful Breadcrumbs.	1 Egg.
¼ teaspoonful Jamaica Pepper.	Salt.

Put the mutton twice through the mincer, add the breadcrumbs, chutney and seasonings and mix very well. Add the egg well beaten and form into a roll and flour it. Lay on a baking dish with some fresh dripping and bake in the oven for an hour basting it frequently. Dish carefully and serve with piquante sauce and orange salad.

IRISH STEW WITH RABBIT. (47)

1 Rabbit.	¾ lb. Onions.
2 lbs. Potatoes.	1 oz. Bacon Fat.
1 teacupful Water.	Salt and Pepper.

Soak and prepare the rabbit as for a stew. Dry it well and cut in neat pieces. Put the bacon fat into a stewpan and make it smoking hot then brown the rabbit quickly in it and keep it hot while the onions are browned lightly.

Have half the potatoes peeled and cut in thick slices and arrange alternate layers of them with the rabbit and onion with seasonings between each.   Pour over the teacupful of water and stew gently for 2 hours.   An hour before serving add the remaining potatoes cut in halves or quarters according to size.   Add more water if necessary, but if the stew is slowly cooked in a stewpan with close fitting lid it should not be required.

If an old rabbit is used and the strong flavour objected to, it should be blanched before browning and cooked longer than a young one.

COLD LAMB CUTLETS.   (48)

6 Cutlets.	2 ozs. Loaf Sugar.
1 gill Vinegar.	½ oz. Powdered Gelatine.
1 gill Boiling Water.	2 tablespoonsful Cold Water.
Handful of Mint.	1 Lettuce.
Cream Dressing.	½ pint Macédoine of Vegetables

Braize the cutlets and press till cold between two dishes with weight on top.

Pound the mint and sugar in a mortar till it becomes a pulp.   Add the boiling water and after it is cold add the vinegar.   Put the gelatine in cold water and stir over the fire till it dissolves, then add it to the mint sauce.   Trim the cutlets neatly and lay in a deep dish or tin which just fits them and be careful to keep all the bones to the left side.   Pour the mint jelly over to entirely cover them and lay aside for some hours till firm.

Arrange a bed of lettuce on an entrée dish and pile the macédoine already mixed with cream dressing in the middle.   Cut out the cutlets from the jelly and arrange round the vegetables, keeping the bones into the centre and finishing with a cutlet frill on each.

LAMB EN CASSEROLE. (49)

2 lbs. best end Neck of Lamb.	1 tablespoonful Chopped Parsley
1 tablespoonful Butter.	2 Tomatoes.
1 large Onion	2 sticks Celery.
½ pint Brown Stock.	1 tablespoonful Flour.
2 teaspoonsful Red Currant Jelly.	4 tablespoonsful Port.
	Salt and Pepper.
1 teaspoonful Chilli Vinegar.	

Melt the butter in a frying pan and add the onion cut in thin slices and fry golden brown, then fry the lamb cut into chops. Put on to a plate and brown the flour, then add stock and make sauce. Put the tomatoes, celery and onion into greased casserole and lay the chops on these. Mix the salt and pepper and vinegar with the sauce and pour over the chops. Lay greased paper over and put on the lid. Cook very slowly in the oven for 2½ hours. Add the wine, red currant jelly and parsley and re-heat to boiling point. Serve in casserole.

When celery is not to be had, tie some celery seed in a scrap of muslin and remove it before serving.

LIVER AND BACON HOT POT. (50)

1 lb. Calf's Liver.	1 oz. Flour.
½ lb. Fat Bacon.	Salt and Pepper.
½ pint Stock.	Pinch of Jamaica Pepper.
2 Onions.	

Scald and dry the onion. Wash the liver in tepid water, dry it and cut in slices about a third of an inch thick. Fry the bacon very lightly and lay aside as it is done. Mix the flour and seasonings on a plate and coat the slices of liver with it then fry in the bacon fat. Put a layer of bacon in a deep hot pot then one of liver, add seasonings and some grated onion and continue in this order till all is used up having bacon for the last layer. Put any remaining flour into the frying pan and brown it then add the stock, boil up, skim and pour over the liver and bacon. Put on a greased paper and then the lid and let it cook *slowly* in the oven for at least 4 hours. Remove the greased paper and serve in the hot pot with a napkin pinned round.

ROAST MUTTON WITH ONIONS. (51)

If you have never eaten mutton roasted with onions you will find that it makes a pleasant variety. Roast the joint in the usual way and cook garden onions round it as you would potatoes. Baste these well along with the roast and serve when cooked in a vegetable dish. They should be whole and a nice brown colour. Both the mutton and the gravy have a much better flavour done in this way. After pouring off the dripping some cooks thicken the gravy with the water that has been drained from the potatoes and it certainly tastes very good.

RABBIT CUTLETS AND ASPARAGUS TIPS. (52)

2 Young Rabbits.	1 tin Asparagus Tips.

Marinade :—

1 Egg well beaten.	1 teaspoonful Lemon Juice
1 oz. Melted Butter.	and pinch of Rind.
1 large teaspoonful Chopped Parsley.	Salt and Pepper.

Fillet as many cutlets as are required from the rabbits and beat them with a wet cutlet bat. Mix the marinade on a plate and let them lie in it for an hour, turning once during that time.

Dip them in dried white crumbs, season with salt and pepper, press into shape and fry in shallow fat. Drain well and serve round a bed composed of asparagus tips.

These should be rinsed and drained and tossed in melted butter with a dust of salt till very hot.

Serve with the following sauce :—

½ pint Rabbit or Veal Stock.	Squeeze of Lemon Juice.
Yolk of 1 Egg.	Salt and Pepper.
¾ oz. Butter.	¾ oz. Flour.

Melt butter and flour and blend together. Add by degrees the stock and beat it all very well. Let it cook gently for 20 minutes. Cool slightly, add the salt and pepper and the yolk then cook for a few minutes but do not let it boil. Add lemon juice just before serving.

SCOTCH HAGGIS. (53)

1 Sheep's Bag and Pluck.	1 pint Stock.
2 teacups Oatmeal.	1 large teacup Suet.
4 medium sized Spanish Onions.	¼ teaspoonful Grated Nutmeg.
½ teaspoonful White Pepper.	¼ teaspoonful Black Pepper.
½ teaspoonful Jamaica Pepper.	2 teaspoonsful Salt or more.

Wash the bag in plenty of cold water then put it into warm water and scrape it till perfectly clean. Let it lie overnight in salted water.

Wash the pluck thoroughly, make an incision in heart and liver and put on in a pan of cold water with the windpipe hanging over the side of the pan. When it boils change the water for clean boiling water, slightly salted, and let it boil 1½ to 2 hours till the liver is tender enough to grate. Take out of the pan and let it get cold then cut away the windpipe and any black pieces.

Meanwhile parboil the onions and toast the oatmeal in front of the fire or in the oven till golden brown. Chop the heart and lungs and grate the liver. Chop the onion and suet finely and mix all these well together with the oatmeal, seasonings and a pint of the liquor in which the

pluck was boiled.   Rather more than half fill the bag with
the mixture, sew up the hole with a needle and strong
cotton and cook slowly in boiling water for 3 hours.   When
the haggis begins to swell prick with large needle to prevent
it bursting.   If there are any thin parts in the bag sew
before filling or it may burst in the pot.

Serve *very* hot on a folded napkin, making an incision
on the top just before sending to table.

Tastes differ very much with regard to seasoning and
most cooks have their own ideas of what is necessary.   The
above quantities are just given as a guide but it is usual to
season a haggis highly.   Haggis can be kept for some time
after cooking in this manner but should be boiled for about
¾ of an hour before serving.

STEAMED STEAK AND GREEN PEA PURÉE.   (54)

1¼ lbs. Steak.	Salt and Spiced Pepper.
1 tablespoonful Flour.	2 tablespoonsful Water.

Have the steak cut in thin slices and then into strips
about 2 inches wide as for pie.   Mix the flour and seasonings on a plate and coat each piece of steak with this and
roll up with a tiny piece of fat on each roll.   Lay loosely
in a pudding basin, add the water and any left over flour,
cover with a greased paper and steam steadily for 3 hours.

Serve in a border of green pea purée.

STEAMED SWEETBREADS.   (55)

2 Sweetbreads.	1 tablespoonful Chopped Parsley.
1 thick Rasher Streaky Bacon.	2 tablespoonsful Flour.
Salt and Pepper.	Grated Rind of ½ Lemon.
Boiled Rice.	1 teaspoonful Vinegar.

Put the sweetbreads into cold water as soon as they are received. Let them soak for 2 hours or longer and change water once or twice. Put in pan of salted boiling water with vinegar and cook slowly for 15 minutes. Put again into cold water then press between 2 plates.

Mix flour, parsley, lemon rind and seasoning on a plate. Remove fat from sweetbreads and cut in neat slices. Cut bacon in blocks and dip all into floury mixture. Put lightly into a basin, add $\frac{1}{2}$ gill water, cover with greased paper and steam $1\frac{1}{2}$ hours. Turn out and dish in a border of well boiled rice. This makes a very good mixture for a vol-au-vent.

SWISS OLIVES. (56)

1 lb. Lean Pork.	1 teacupful Breadcrumbs.
$\frac{3}{4}$ pint Brown Stock.	$\frac{1}{2}$ teaspoonful Powdered Sage.
1 Egg.	Salt and Pepper.
Flour.	Browning.
$\frac{1}{4}$ pint Apple Sauce.	

Mix the breadcrumbs and sage together. Put the pork through the mincer and mix it with the breadcrumbs. Beat the egg well and add to the mixture. Season and form into balls about the size of a walnut and flour them well. Have the stock, which should be made from pork bones if possible, boiling and add the olives. Allow them to stew gently for an hour, then thicken the stock with $\frac{1}{2}$ an ounce of flour broken in a little cold water. Season well and add a few drops of browning to improve the colour and strain over the olives. Serve with apple sauce handed separately.

COLD MEAT COOKERY.

COLD ROUND OF BEEF IN SHERRY. (57)

½ lb. Cold Round of Beef.
2 teacupsful Sherry.
2 tablespoonsful Worcester
    Sauce.

1½ ozs. Butter.
1 scant teaspoonful Jamaica
    Pepper.
1 teaspoonful Potato Flour.

Cut the beef in thin slices. Mix the pepper and sherry together in a pie dish and lay the beef in it. Let it soak one hour, turning it once during that time. Heat the butter in a stew pan. Drip slices of the beef and fry in the butter. As it is done lay on a dish and keep hot over boiling water. When all the beef has been fried add the potato flour to the butter, stir up the sherry mixture and add it. Let it all boil up, then return the beef to the sauce and keep it below boiling point for 20 minutes. Dish up the meat, take the saucepan from the fire and add the Worcester sauce and pour all over the beef. Serve boiled rice separately. The Worcester sauce should not be allowed to cook in the sherry.

CROMARTY CUTLETS. (58)

1 teacupful Porridge.
8 ozs. Cooked Meat.
1 teaspoonful Chopped
    Parsley.
Salt and Pepper.
Egg and Breadcrumbs.

½ oz. Butter.
1 teaspoonful Mushroom
    Ketchup.
½ small Spanish Onion.
Flour.

Put the meat through the mincer. Scald the Spanish onion and grate it. Melt the butter in a saucepan and fry the onion in it till cooked, add the meat, porridge and seasonings and mix thoroughly. Turn on to a plate and spread out to cool. Form into balls and then with a knife dipped in flour shape into cutlets. Dip these into well seasoned egg and breadcrumbs and fry a nice brown. Serve very hot with a good sauce.

The porridge should not be at all sloppy otherwise it will not bind the cutlets sufficiently.

HASH. (59)

To make a good hash it is necessary to make a good sauce with fried onion and a few vegetables cut up small and some good stock, thickening it with 1 oz. flour to the pint of stock. If the meat to be hashed is mutton 1 teaspoonful of chutney to the pint is a great improvement. Let the sauce simmer for an hour and strain it. When it is quite cold, add the meat and heat to boiling point and serve at once. Garnish with macaroni, rice, or sippets of toast. The chief point is to see that the meat goes into cold sauce and not into hot, as is usually done, and that it is not allowed to boil.

TO CURRY TINNED RABBIT. (60)

1 tin Rabbit.	Large Onion.
¾ pint Stock.	1 oz. Flour.
1 dessertspoonful Curry Powder.	1 Apple.
1 teaspoonful Chutney.	1 oz. Margarine.
Salt.	Lemon Juice.
Boiled Rice.	

This is an exceedingly economical dish and, if the following directions are carefully carried out, a most appetising one.

Open the tin and remove the rabbit to a dish. Take off all the jelly adhering to it and measure it for the stock, adding enough hot water to make up the quantity required. Peel and slice the onion finely and fry it in the margarine for 5 minutes. Add the curry powder and the apple chopped up and fry another 5 minutes, then add flour and mix well. Add the stock by degrees, beating the sauce free from lumps. When it boils add the chutney and salt and let it simmer for an hour or an hour and a half. Meanwhile cut the rabbit off the bones into neat pieces and add it to the sauce. Let it heat to boiling point, but on no account let it boil or continue cooking after the rabbit is added. Add lemon juice to taste and serve very hot with well boiled rice handed separately.

SWEETBREAD CUTLETS AND CURRY SAUCE. (61)

4 tablespoons Cooked Sweet- breads.	1 oz. Flour.
6 small Mushrooms.	1 oz. Margarine.
¼ teaspoonful Curry Powder.	1 gill Stock or Milk.
1 yolk of Egg.	1 tablespoonful Cream.
½ teaspoonful Chutney.	Lemon Juice.
Salt and Pepper.	Egg and Breadcrumbs.

Chop up any left over sweetbread. Peel the mushrooms and chop up finely. Make a thick sauce with the flour, margarine and stock ; add the curry powder and chutney, and cook 10 minutes. Let it cool a little and add the cream, a dash of lemon juice, and the yolk of egg. Mix well and add sweetbread and mushrooms. When cold form into cutlets, dip in egg and breadcrumbs and fry a golden brown in deep fat. Serve on a bed of mashed potatoes with curry sauce poured round.

MISCELLANEOUS BREAKFAST, LUNCHEON AND SUPPER DISHES.

STEWED BEEF HAM. (62)

This is an old fashioned country dish and very savoury it will be found.

1 lb. raw Beef Ham, very thinly sliced.	Salt and Pepper.
2 Onions.	1 tablespoonful Bacon Fat or Butter.
1 dessertspoonful Flour.	1 gill Water.

Heat the fat in a stew pan. Mix the flour and seasonings, dip the slices of ham in it and fry lightly in the fat ; as each slice is done put on a dish and keep hot. Slice the onions thinly and fry a golden brown. Return the ham to the stew pan, add the water and stew very gently for 1½ to 2 hours. Serve with 3 ozs. of boiled macaroni as a garnish.

" BOBOTEE." (63)

This Indian dish is very useful as any kind of cooked or tinned meat can be used for it. If tinned rabbit or corned beef are used, it makes a most economical dish. Cooked, chilled tripe is also excellent done in this way.

1 lb. Cooked Meat.	1 gill Milk.
1 thick slice Bread.	1 dessertspoonful Curry Powder.
2 Eggs.	Juice of ½ a Lemon.
2 Onions.	1 oz. Margarine.
Salt.	

Soak the bread in water and put the meat through mincer. Slice the onions in very thin rings and fry in the margarine for 10 minutes, add the curry powder and fry another 10 minutes till onions are soft. Squeeze the water out of the bread, mix with the minced meat then add the onion and mix all very thoroughly. Season and add lemon juice and put into a pie dish. Pour over the eggs, well beaten and mixed with the milk and bake in a good oven for half an hour. A teaspoonful of good chutney is a great improvement.

BRAIN CROQUETTES. (64)

2 Sets of Brains.	1 slice Onion.
Panada—1 oz. Butter.	1 tablespoonful Chopped
1 oz. Flour.	Parsley.
1 gill Milk.	Salt and Pepper.
	Egg and Breadcrumbs.

Wash the brains and let them soak for half an hour in salt and water. Then put them on in a saucepan with a slice of onion and a pinch of salt and bring to the boil. Boil gently for 10 minutes. Drain, skin and cut into tiny dice. Make a panada or thick sauce with the ingredients given and season it very well. Add the brains, mix and turn on to a plate to cool. Form into rolls with a floured knife. Dip in egg and breadcrumbs and fry a golden brown in deep fat. Serve with piquante sauce.

BRUSSELS SPROUT FRITTERS. (65)

1 dozen large Sprouts.	Breadcrumbs.
½ lb. Pork Sausages.	Flour.
Milk.	Seasonings.

Choose large, firm, close-leaved sprouts of equal size. Trim them and let them lie in salt and water for an hour or two. Remove the skins from the sausages and divide into twelve parts. Cook the sprouts till tender in salted boiling water, drain well and completely mask them in the sausage meat.

Mix some flour with a little milk to a smooth cream, add some salt and pepper and dip each sprout in it. Toss in breadcrumbs and fry in deep fat. Drain and serve on a bed of mashed potatoes with vegetarian brown sauce.

STUFFED CABBAGE. (66)

1 Savoy Cabbage.

STUFFING.

6 ozs. Cooked Meat.	1 tablespoonful Chopped Parsley.
4 ozs. Sausage Meat.	½ Onion, grated.
Gravy.	
2 tablespoonsful Breadcrumbs.	

1 Onion.	½ pint Stock.
1 Carrot.	½ pint Brown Sauce.

Prepare the cabbage as for boiling. Remove the stalk and cook it for 10 minutes. With a sharp knife cut out the heart from the stalk end. Prepare the stuffing and make nicely moist with a little gravy. Put a little of it between the leaves of the cabbage, dividing it equally all round. Replace as much of the heart as possible and tie with a string. Lay it in a fireproof baking dish with the stock and add the onion and carrot sliced. Put it into a good oven, cover with a piece of greased paper and bake for 1½ hours basting very frequently with the stock.

When done pour off the stock, reduce it, then add it to the brown sauce. Remove the string from the cabbage and pour sauce round.

CHEESE PUFFER. (67)

1 breakfastcup Grated Cheese.	Pinch of Cayenne.
Whites of two Eggs.	Salt and Pepper.

Put the whites of egg into a basin and beat till very stiff. Mix the seasonings with the cheese and fold into the beaten whites. Do not stir this mixture, but with a plated table-spoon take spoonsful and turn over gently till all is well mixed together. Heap up on a greased fireproof dish and bake in a hot oven for 10 minutes. Send to table with all possible speed.

STEWED CHESTNUTS. (68)

1½ lbs. Chestnuts.	1 Onion.
¾ pint Brown Stock.	¾ oz. Flour.
1 oz. Butter.	Salt and Pepper.

A few drops Browning if necessary.

Slit and boil chestnuts for 15 minutes and remove both skins. Melt the butter in a stewpan and add the onion which should be scalded and grated and let them cook together for a few minutes. Add the flour and brown slowly. Thin down by degrees with the stock and add the chestnuts. Let all stew till tender. They will take about 35 to 45 minutes. Season well and if necessary add a few drops of browning to improve the colour.

FRENCH PIE. (69)

1½ lbs. Calf's Liver.	⅓ lb. Unsmoked Fat Bacon.
1 Shallot.	¼ lb. Sausage Meat.
Pinch of Cayenne and Mace.	1 pint Good Stock.
½ teaspoonful Black Pepper.	1½ ozs. Gelatine.

Boil the liver and when cold mince it twice. Pound with the seasonings. Line a mould with thin slices of the at bacon, then a thin layer of sausage meat and a thick one of liver. Continue till dish is full. Dissolve gelatine in the stock and pour over. Put a layer of bacon on top. Bake 2 hours in a moderate oven. Turn out when cold.

ITALIAN PIE. (70)

A thoroughly appetising and economical dish can be prepared from fresh or left over corned beef in the following manner.

4 ozs. Macaroni.	1 small tin Tomatoes (skinned).
¾ lb. Corned Beef.	2 small or 1 large Onion.
Breadcrumbs.	Salt and Pepper.
½ oz. Margarine.	

Break the macaroni in convenient lengths and boil till tender in salted water. Scald the onion in a small basin of boiling water to which a piece of soda the size of a pea has been added, for ten minutes, rinse it, dry and cut in slices. Fry till slightly brown in the margarine. Put the corned beef through the mincer and grease a pie dish. Arrange a layer of macaroni, then one of fried onion, then tomato and then corned beef, adding a dust of salt and pepper between each. Repeat till all is used up, having macaroni at the top. Cover with breadcrumbs and dot a few pieces of margarine on top. Bake in good oven for 40 minutes. If the tomatoes are not juicy add any gravy that is at hand so that the pie will be sufficiently moist.

Cold beef, or a mixture of cold cooked meats may be used for this dish.

KIDNEYS COOKED IN THEIR FAT.   (71)

This method of cooking kidneys makes a pleasant variety for breakfast.   Take 3 fresh sheep's kidneys and cut in rounds half an inch thick but don't remove the fat. Dip in cream seasoned with salt and pepper and a squeeze of lemon juice.   Toss in seasoned flour and fry till brown on each side in bacon fat.   Serve on rounds of toast or fried bread.

Milk thickened to the consistency of cream with a little flour may be used when cream is not at hand.

KIDNEY ROLLS.   (72)

1 Sheep's Kidney.	Fried Bread.
6 Rashers of Bacon.	

STUFFING.

1 teacupful Breadcrumbs.	Cook's Egg.
½ small Onion.	Pinch of Lemon Rind.
1 teaspoonful Chopped Parsley.	Salt and Pepper.

Skin the kidney and cut it into small pieces.   Divide these pieces into six portions.   Sieve the soft breadcrumbs into a basin add the lemon rind the parsley very finely chopped and the onion grated.   Season well with salt and spiced pepper and bind with some Cook's egg.   Choose rashers of bacon which are rather broad and not very lean, spread each with the stuffing then add a portion of the kidney nicely seasoned and roll up neatly.   Run two fine skewers or hat pins through the rolls and lay on a Yorkshire tin and bake in a good oven for 20 minutes.   Serve very hot on oval pieces of fried bread.   Care should be taken not to overcook the bacon ; it should be nicely browned and not at all hard.

LEEK PIE. (73)

10 Leeks.	1½ gills Milk.
1 yolk of Egg.	2 tablespoonsful Cream.
1 teaspoonful Cornflour.	Walnut of Butter.
Salt and Pepper.	Short Crust.

Wash the leeks carefully, prepare as for boiling and tie in bundles. Boil in salted water for 20 minutes and drain very well. Cut in 2 inch lengths and lay in a greased pie-dish.

Heat the milk and butter and when it boils add the cornflour and let it cook for a few minutes. Season well and cool slightly then add the cream and yolk of egg and pour over the leeks. Cover with a good short crust and bake for half an hour.

MACARONI AND HAM. (74)

4 ozs. Macaroni.	1 teacupful Fried Ham.
1 Egg.	Salt and Pepper.
½ pint White Sauce.	Breadcrumbs.
½ oz. Margarine.	

Boil the macaroni and drain it well. Make the white sauce, cool slightly and add the egg well beaten. Mince the ham and add it with the macaroni. Mix well and season to taste. Pour into a greased pie dish, cover with bread crumbs and dot some pieces of margarine on top. Bake in a moderate oven till the crumbs are nicely browned—from 20 to 30 minutes.

MACARONI AND PEAS. (75)

This is an exceedingly nourishing lunch or supper dish.

4 ozs. Macaroni.	Small nut of Butter.
½ pint White Sauce.	A sprig of Mint.
4 ozs. Grated Cheese.	¼ teaspoonful Made Mustard.
1 bottle or tin of Peas.	Salt and Pepper.

Boil the macaroni in salted water till quite tender and leave to drain. Add to the white sauce and re-heat, then add the mustard and the cheese and mix well. Rinse the peas, re-heat in the butter, adding the mint and keeping the saucepan lid on till heated. Make a border of the macaroni and cheese, fill the centre with the peas and dust with pepper. Serve at once.—Fresh peas should be used when possible or, if a less expensive dish is wanted, dried peas may be used ; they should be well soaked and no salt added to them in cooking till they are quite soft.

MOCK HAGGIS. (76)

8 ozs. Cooked Meat.	2 Onions (grated).
1 teacupful Oatmeal.	Salt, Pepper and Jamaica
½ pint Stock.	Pepper.
2 ozs. Suet.	

Chop the suet very finely. Mince the meat and toast the oatmeal till it becomes pale brown. Mix all well together. Add the onions seasonings and stock. Turn into a greased bowl and steam for 3 hours. Serve with a napkin pinned round the bowl.

MOCK SOLE. (77)

½ pint Milk.	1 teaspoonful grated Onion.
1¾ ozs. Semolina.	Pinch of Powdered Mace.
1 oz. Butter.	1 teaspoonful Lemon Juice.
2 large Potatoes.	¼ Rind of Lemon, grated.
Salt and Pepper.	Egg and Breadcrumbs.

Boil and mash the potatoes very well. Boil milk and onion, add semolina, butter and seasonings and then potatoes *while hot*. Cook for a few minutes. Spread out on flat dish to cool. Arrange like fillets of sole. Egg and crumb and fry in deep fat. Serve with parsley sauce handed separately and garnish the fillets with lemon.

PICKLED PORK AND TONGUE.   (78)

Procure a piece of pork and a pig's tongue which have been in the pickle only a few days.   The pork should be about 12 inches square or thereabouts so that it is sufficiently large to encase the tongue.

Wash and dry these and lay on a board then dust the pork with Jamaica pepper and powdered sage.   Lay the tongue on this and roll up firmly.   Bind it well with tape and put it into tepid water.   When it comes to the boil skim it and let it simmer gently from 3 to 3½ hours according to size.

Let it get two-thirds cool in the water then press between two dishes (with the join underneath) and a weight on top.   When quite cold remove the tape, garnish neatly and serve for breakfast.

PIG IN A POKE.   (79)

This most savoury method of cooking potatoes was first suggested by the late Alexis Soyer whose cooking delighted the members of the Reform Club nearly a century ago.

Take eight potatoes of not less than 4 ozs. weight and peel them.   With an apple corer make a hole lengthwise through each.   Dust the hole lightly with salt and fill the cavity with sausage meat which may be flavoured with sage if liked.   Melt some good dripping in a strong pan and when it gets hot put in the potatoes, put on a lid and cook steadily till tender.   Turn the potatoes from time to time and dust with fine salt.   Serve very hot.

If potatoes of this size are used they should be cooked in 45 to 50 minutes.

These potatoes are also good baked in the oven without any fat and may be served with brown gravy. They will take about 1½ to 2 hours to bake without dripping. Half an ounce of sausage meat is sufficient for each potato.

GALANTINE OF RABBIT.   (80)

¾ lb. Rabbit.	2 hard Boiled Eggs.
½ lb. Bacon.	6 ozs. Breadcrumbs.
Grated Rind of ½ Lemon.	1 Egg.
1 dessertspoonful Chopped Parsley.	1 gill Stock.
	Pinch of Mace.
Salt and Pepper.	Pinch of Jamaica Pepper.

Remove the required amount of meat from two rabbits which have been thoroughly cleaned. Put the rabbit and bacon twice through the mincer. Mix the bread crumbs with the seasonings and add the meat to them. Mix very well. Beat up the egg and add the stock to it and mix thoroughly with the dry ingredients. Lay mixture out flat and arrange the eggs, cut in half, upon it and roll up tightly in a floured cloth. Tie the ends firmly and put into boiling water flavoured with a few vegetables and boil gently for 2 hours. Take it out, let the steam escape and roll it in a clean cloth. Press between two flat dishes with a light weight on top and when it is cold brush with tomato glaze and garnish nicely.

RABBIT HOT POT.   (81)

1 Rabbit.	2 tablespoonsful Breadcrumbs.
¼ lb. Bacon.	1 tablespoonful Chopped Parsley.
1 Egg.	
½ pint Stock.	1 oz. Flour.
Pinch of Lemon Rind.	

Wash and soak the rabbit in salt and water for ½ an hour after carefully removing the gall from the liver.

Parboil the heart and liver, and chop very finely, and mix with the breadcrumbs, parsley, lemon rind, salt and pepper. Bind with the egg, well beaten, and form into balls. Put a layer of bacon in a hot pot, then one of rabbit cut in neat pieces and floured, season, add a layer of forcemeat balls, and repeat till all is used up. Cover with the stock and cook in a moderate oven for two hours. If the rabbits are young they will cook in an hour. Serve in the hot pot with a napkin pinned round.

POTTED RABBIT.   (82)

1 Rabbit.	Salt and Pepper.
Butter.	Pinch of Ground Mace.

Wash and soak the rabbit in the usual way. Dry well and cut in small pieces. Lay it in a covered jar with a greased paper on top and set it in a saucepan with boiling water to come half way up and steam steadily for 3 hours, or less if the rabbit is very young. No water or stock of any kind should be added to the rabbit. Remove the meat from the bones and pound in a mortar with butter, using 4 ozs. to each ½ lb. of meat. Season very well, using mace if the flavour is liked, then stir in the juice which has come from the rabbit in cooking. Mix very well and when quite cold put into pots and cover with clarified butter. If liked the paste may be passed through a fine sieve before potting but this does not tend to improve the flavour.

RED POTTAGE.   (83)

½ lb. Butter Beans.	1 lb. Tomatoes.
½ lb. Bacon.	2 quarts Cold Water.
1 Onion.	Pepper and Salt.

Wash beans well and soak overnight in the cold water. Boil in this water next day and add one onion, but no salt. They will take from 1½ ro 2 hours. Drain and remove onion. (The water should be set aside for stock). Peel and slice tomatoes and remove rind from bacon. Cover the bottom of a fairly deep earthenware dish with rashers of bacon, cover with beans and then with tomato and season the last mentioned layers. Repeat till all is used up and have bacon last. Put a greased paper on top and then the lid and bake in a moderate oven for 3 hours. It must not be allowed to cook fast or the flavour will be spoiled and it will dry up. Tinned tomatoes may be used when more convenient.

SANDWICH ROLL.   (84)

This is a quickly made and inexpensive roll useful for making sandwiches or for odd snacks :—

6 ozs. Sausages (Pork).	1 teacup Breadcrumbs.
4 ozs. Ham or Bacon.	½ teacup Milk.
1 Cook's Farm Egg.	Salt and Pepper.
Pinch of Ground Mace.	¼ teaspoonful Onion Powder.

Put the bacon through the mincer. Skin the sausages and mix these together with a fork. Add the breadcrumbs and seasonings and mix. Beat the egg after preparing it as directed on the package and add to the milk. Then mix all together.

Grease a straight-necked 2 lb. jam pot liberally and into this press the mixture. Cover with a greased paper and steam for 2 hours.

Let it stand for a minute to shrink before turning out and then roll at once in golden brown breadcrumbs.

SARDINE CUTLETS. (85)

4 ozs. Sardines.	1 Egg.
½ oz. Butter.	½ teaspoon Lemon Juice.
½ oz. Flour.	White Breadcrumbs.
½ gill Water.	Fried Parsley.
Salt and Cayenne.	

Skin, bone and chop up the sardines finely with a silver knife. Melt butter in a saucepan, add flour, mix and then add water. Cook till the mixture leaves the sides of the pan clean. Remove from the fire, add the sardines (which should be weighed after preparing), seasonings and lemon juice. Mix very well and turn on to a plate to cool. Form into small balls of equal size and then into small cutlets. Dip in egg and breadcrumbs and fry a golden brown. Drain well and dish up with the fried parsley as a garnish.

SAUSAGES AND APPLE SAUCE. (86)

1 lb. Pork Sausages.	1 Cabbage.
1 Egg.	Breadcrumbs.
1 teaspoonful Powdered Sage.	½ pint Apple Sauce.
½ oz. Butter.	New Potatoes.

Prick the sausages and par-boil for 10 minutes, then remove the skins. Season the egg and crumbs with sage, salt and pepper. Egg and crumb and fry in deep fat. Make a neat mound of the cabbage which should be boiled and finely chopped with the butter and seasoned well. Dish the sausages on this. Garnish with parsley and tiny new potatoes which should be cooked in a strong pan with lid in pork dripping or butter till golden brown and dusted with fine salt. They will take from 15 to 20 minutes, according to size. Hand the apple sauce separately.

SAUSAGES AND TOMATO SAUCE. (87)

1 lb. Sausages.	1 tablespoonful Onion Juice.
½ pint Sieved Tomato.	1 teaspoonful Rice Flour.
Salt and Pepper.	Sippets of Toast.

Wash the sausages and prick very well indeed with a fork to prevent them bursting. Lay in a frying pan and cover with boiling water slightly salted. Let them cook gently with a lid on for 15 minutes then remove the lid and allow the water to boil away and the sausages to brown nicely. Mix the sieved tomato and onion juice together and blend the rice flour carefully with it. Pour this into the frying pan and stir about till it boils. Season well then cover and let the tomatoes and sausage simmer for 10 minutes, then serve garnished with sippets of toast.

TOAD-IN-A-HOLE WITH SAUSAGES. (88)

1 lb. Cambridge Sausages.

½ lb. Flour.	2 Eggs.
1 pint Milk.	Salt and Pepper.

Sieve flour into a basin and add salt and pepper. Make a hole in the centre and break in the eggs. Stir with a wooden spoon and add by degrees enough milk to make a thick paste which must be beaten quite free from lumps. Add a little more milk as it gets smooth and when it gets to a nice beating consistency beat for 15 minutes. Then add the remainder of the milk and let it stand for at least an hour before cooking.

Par-boil the sausages for 5 minutes. Remove the skins and cut in half lengthways. Grease a large pie dish or Yorkshire tin liberally and arrange sausages on it. Pour the batter over and bake for ¾ of an hour in a steady oven. The success of this dish depends upon the thorough beating of the batter and allowing it to stand before cooking.

SAVOURY TOMATO CUSTARDS. (89)

2 Eggs.	1½ ozs. grated Cheese.
1½ gills Milk.	Salt, Pepper and Cayenne.
1 gill Tomato Purée.	

Beat the eggs, add the milk and sieved tomato pulp, which should be warmed together, but must not boil. Add the grated cheese and seasoning to taste. Mix well and pour into greased ramequin dishes or a small pie dish. Bake in a steady oven 10 to 15 minutes for the small custards, or 40 to 50 for the large. The custard should be just set.

These custards can be steamed if more suitable. Cover with greased paper and steam same length of time.

TOMATO AND MUSHROOM ENTRÉE. (90)

6 Mushrooms.	½ pint White Sauce.
3 Tomatoes.	2 hard boiled Eggs.
Potato Border.	1 raw Egg.
Butter.	Parsley and Herbs.
Salt and Pepper.	White Breadcrumbs.

Choose tomatoes and mushrooms of even size. Skin the tomatoes, which should be quite firm, and cut in halves. Beat up the egg and season it well with salt and pepper, chopped parsley and powdered herbs. Flour the halved tomatoes, dip in the egg, toss in dry white breadcrumbs and fry a golden brown.

Peel the mushrooms and bake with a little butter on a greased baking dish for 10 minutes in a steady oven. Make the white sauce rather thick and add the hard boiled eggs roughly chopped. Dish the tomatoes and mushrooms alternately on the border of mashed potato and fill the centre with the egg sauce. Garnish with parsley and serve very hot.

FRIED TRIPE. (91)

Many people have overcome prejudices with regard to foodstuffs during the last five years, and perhaps more with frozen foods than others. Tripe is a favourite dish in many households, but hitherto it has meant so much trouble for the cook that it has often been avoided.

Frozen tripe arrives in one's kitchen cooked and only requires to be thawed for 12 to 24 hours, thoroughly washed in cold water and cooked for a short time to make it beautifully tender. Anything approaching fast boiling must be avoided, as it quickly hardens it.

A pleasant variety can be had by frying the tripe in the following manner.

Take 1¼ lbs. tripe, thaw, wash and cut up in neat pieces about 2 inches square. Put it on in a stewpan of cold water and let it come slowly to the boil. Add 3 onions of medium size, cut in half. Let this simmer gently for 1½ hours and add salt half an hour before it is done. Prepare a batter with

4 ozs. Flour.	1 gill Milk and Water.
1 Egg.	Salt and Pepper.

and let it stand for an hour. Drain the tripe thoroughly, dip in the batter and fry a golden brown in deep fat. Dish neatly on a border of mashed potato and pour round ½ pint of good white sauce to which has been added the onion boiled with the tripe and sieved. A still greater variety is given if tomato sauce is substituted for onion sauce.

VEGETABLE CURRY. (92)

1 pint Cooked Vegetables.	Salt.
½ gill Cocoanut Milk.	½ pint Stock.
1 oz. Butter.	1 Apple.
1 oz. Flour.	2 Onions.
1 dessertspoonful Curry	1 teaspoonful Chutney.
Powder.	1 dessertspoonful Lemon Juice.

Use any vegetables that are in season and cut them in neat pieces. If liked a proportion of haricot or butter beans may be included but these should be cooked separately.

Melt the butter in a stewpan or fireproof casserole and add the onions chopped. Let them cook slowly till golden brown then add the apple also chopped and cook 5 minutes. Heat the flour and the curry powder in the oven for 10 minutes and then add these. Let them cook together *very* slowly till the butter is absorbed and stir well to prevent burning. Add the chutney and by degrees the stock and let all cook gently for 1 hour. Add the cocoanut milk and cook 1½ hours more. Have the vegetables well drained and add to the sauce and let all cook very gently for another hour. Add salt to taste and just before serving add the lemon juice. Serve boiled rice in a separate dish and hand cut lemon with the curry.

One of the chief points in making a good curry is the slow cooking of the powder before thinning down and the long slow cooking after.

CURRIED VEGETABLE MARROW. (93)

1 Marrow.	1 tablespoonful Curry Powder.
2 Onions.	½ an Apple.
1 oz. Flour.	1 pint Stock.
1 teaspoonful Lemon Juice.	1 oz. Margarine.
2 teaspoonsful Chutney.	Salt.

STUFFING.

¾ lb. Cold Meat.	1 slice Bread.
2 level teaspoonsful Curry Powder.	1 Egg.
	Salt.

Slice the onions thinly and fry in the margarine. Add the tablespoonful curry powder and the apple and fry also. Then add the flour, and, by degrees, the stock and the chutney. Let it simmer for half an hour, then add the salt. Peel the marrow, which should be a medium sized one. Cut it in four and remove the seeds. Soak the bread in the milk, mix the meat, which should be finely minced, with the curry powder, and add to the bread. Season with salt and bind with the beaten egg. Fill up the pieces of marrow with this stuffing, then flour them well and stew gently in the curry sauce till tender, from 35 to 45 minutes. Before serving add the lemon juice to the sauce and serve with well boiled rice handed separately.

For those who do not like a hot curry less powder may be used but curry powders vary very much in strength.

EGG DISHES.

ANCHOVY ROLLS. (94)

This dish is very popular in Lincolnshire where the country people make it with the tops of cottage loaves and call it " Roof."

2 Morning Rolls.	2 hard boiled Eggs.
1 Dessertspoonful Anchovy Essence.	Pepper. Butter.

Boil the Eggs for 20 minutes and put in cold water. Split the rolls and remove the soft dough. Spread both sides of cut pieces liberally with butter. Shell the eggs and chop finely and mix with the anchovy. Season with pepper and spread on the rolls. Cover with the tops and bake in a fairly hot oven till hot and crisp. Cut each into 3 and serve very hot.

BAKED EGGS WITH ARTICHOKES. (95)

4 Eggs.	1½ gills White Sauce.
1 teacupful Cooked Jerusalem Artichokes.	Salt and Pepper. Breadcrumbs and Margarine.
1 oz. Grated Cheese.	

Grease a pie-dish and cover with the artichokes cut in slices. Have the sauce boiling and well seasoned and add the cheese to it. Pour half of it over the artichokes then drop in 4 quite fresh eggs. Dust with salt and pepper and pour the remainder of the sauce over. Dust with bread crumbs and dot over some margarine. Bake for 10 minutes in a good oven.

CABBAGE AND EGGS. (96)

For a light lunch or supper dish take 2 or 3 spring cabbages according to the size, and boil till tender in salted water. Drain and press between two plates with a weight on top to remove all water. Pass through a sieve and re-heat with 2 tablespoons cream and a little spiced pepper. Form into a bed on a hot dish and lay well drained poached eggs on top. Allow one egg for each person and garnish with fried croutons of bread.

CODDLED EGGS. (97)

When eggs are cheap it is well to make use of them in the daily menu as much as possible. If you have never tried an egg cooked in this way you will be surprised to find how light it is. Put the egg to be boiled into a saucepan of absolutely boiling water and put on the lid. Remove the saucepan to the side of the fire where it won't boil, and allow the egg to remain in it 5 to 6 minutes, according to size and freshness. The white should be soft and creamy, and the yolk, of course, quite soft and running. The albumen in the egg does not harden in this way of cooking as it does when the egg is boiled and it is consequently very easily digested. If several eggs are done at once, use a much larger quantity of water, and allow a minute more for cooking.

EGGS À LA MARTIN. (98)

6 New Laid Eggs.	1½ ozs. Cheese.
¾ oz. Flour.	½ pint Milk.
¾ oz. Butter.	Salt and Pepper.

Grease a fireproof baking dish or flat pie dish and grate the cheese. Make a sauce of the flour, butter and milk, and season it well. Pour half of the sauce into the baking dish, quickly break the eggs and lay carefully on the top. Cover with the remainder of the sauce, which should be kept boiling, and sprinkle the grated cheese on top. Bake in a good oven for 5 minutes and serve at once.

EGGS FRIED IN BATTER. (99)

6 Eggs.

Batter—2 ozs. Flour.	1½ tablespoonsful Milk.
2 Eggs.	1 tablespoonful Salad Oil.
Lemon Juice.	Salt and Pepper.
Fried Parsley.	

Poach 6 eggs carefully in salted water to which some lemon juice has been added. When cooked lift out on a fish slice and trim neatly and lay aside on a dish to get cold.

Batter.—Sieve the flour into a basin add salt and the yolks of the eggs and mix very thoroughly. By degrees add milk and salad oil beating very vigorously till all is perfectly smooth. Whip the whites of the eggs very stiffly and just before frying mix lightly into the batter.

Dust the poached eggs with salt and pepper and dip each one carefully into the batter and coat well over. Slip into a pan of smoking fat and fry till golden brown. Drain and serve neatly garnished with fried parsley. These eggs are delicious but need very careful handling as the eggs in the first instance should not be poached at all hard.

EGG AND POTATO PIE.   (100)

4 Hard Boiled Eggs.	½ lb. Cooked Potato.
1 gill Parsley Sauce.	1½ ozs. Grated Cheese.
2 tablespoonsful Hot Milk.	½ oz. Butter.
Salt and Pepper.	

Sieve the potatoes and put them into a saucepan in which the butter has just been melted and mix together. Re-heat, then add the hot milk and two-thirds of the cheese and beat over the fire till very light.

Grease a pie-dish and put in a layer of potato and then the eggs cut in quarters and mixed with the sauce. Cover with the remainder of the potato, smooth it neatly then sprinkle over the remainder of the cheese and bake in a moderate oven till nicely browned.

FRIED EGGS.   (101)

Those people who object to fried eggs being turned will find this American method very useful when fat is not too plentiful. Measure into a small jug a good teaspoonful of cold water for each egg. Make the fat hot in a frying pan, draw aside and quickly put in the eggs and dust with salt and pepper. Pour the water round the sides of the pan, put on lid and set on the stove again. The eggs will be found to be equally done with no hard edges.

HAM AND EGG ROLLS.   (102)

2 ozs. Cooked Ham.	1 dessertspoonful Chopped
1 oz. Butter.	Parsley.
1 oz. Flour.	Pinch of Grated Nutmeg.
1 gill Milk.	2 Eggs.
Salt and Pepper.	Egg and Breadcrumbs.
1 tablespoonful Cream.	

Boil the eggs for 20 minutes and put them into cold water. Blend the butter and flour over the fire and make into a thick sauce with the milk. Add the cream (or if more convenient use ½ oz. extra butter) and let it cook for a few minutes. Add parsley and cook a few minutes more. Add the ham finely chopped and the eggs more roughly chopped, then the seasonings. Mix well and turn on to a plate to cool. Form into cork-shaped rolls and flour them. Dip in beaten egg and seasoned bread crumbs and fry a golden brown. Serve with tomato sauce handed separately.

MANHATTAN EGGS. (103)

1 gill Onion Purée.	½ gill Milk.
1 oz. Butter.	1 oz. Flour.
4 Eggs.	1 teaspoonful Chopped Parsley.
Salt and Pepper.	

Boil the eggs for 20 minutes and put into cold water. Melt the butter in a saucepan, add the flour, and blend together. Add the onion purée and then by degrees the milk. Let it cook 10 minutes and add parsley and seasonings. Peel the eggs, cut in slices and add to the sauce. Serve in shells with a dust of corraline pepper on top.

NEWPORT EGGS. (104)

3 hard-boiled Eggs.	½ pint Parsley Sauce.
6 rounds of Toast.	6 Rashers of Bacon.

Boil the eggs for 20 minutes, cool in cold water and remove the yolks. Chop the whites and add to the parsley sauce which should not be too thin. Divide between the rounds of toast. Press the yolks through a fine sieve and place in heaps on the toast.

Cut each rasher of bacon in three, roll up, fix on a thin skewer and place in the oven for a few minutes. Garnish the toast with these and serve very hot.

ŒUFS SUR LE PLAT.   (105)

Nothing could be more simple or delicious than this French method of cooking eggs.

A flat, oval or round fireproof " ear dish " is the best thing to cook them in.   Melt half an ounce of butter in an ear dish but do not allow it to get hot or brown.   Drop in four fresh eggs separately.   Dust with pepper and salt and put in the oven till the white is just set.   Place the dish on a hot ashet with a paper between and serve at once with a sprig of parsley as a garnish.

If more convenient, the eggs can be done quite nicely on the top of the range but they must not be allowed to cook fast, nor the yolks to get at all hard.

SCRAMBLED EGGS AND ASPARAGUS. (106)

This is a simple way of using up left over asparagus :—

4 Eggs.	$\frac{1}{2}$ oz. Butter.
4 tablespoons Milk.	2 tablespoonsful Asparagus.
Salt and Pepper.	Round of Toast.

Cut up the asparagus in small pieces.   Melt the butter in a small saucepan, beat the eggs and mix with the milk. Add the asparagus and pepper and salt and stir over the fire till thick and creamy then serve on rounds of buttered toast.

SOUTHPORT EGGS.   (107)

4 New Laid Eggs.	$\frac{3}{4}$ gill Picked Shrimps.
1 gill White Sauce.	Salt and Pepper.

Make the sauce and add the shrimps to it and season. Butter a flat fireproof dish and lay the mixture on it. Break the eggs carefully on top of this.   Dust with salt and pepper and a few breadcrumbs and put into the oven till the eggs are just set.

VEGETABLES AND SALADS.

BEETROOT HOLLANDAISE. (108)

It seems a pity that one so often meets beetroot in this country swimming in a dish of vinegar or boiled and served whole with a starchy white sauce. The Dutch people have a method of serving this valuable vegetable which is a delicious accompaniment to cold mutton, etc. To prepare it wash a couple of beetroots carefully without breaking the skin and boil from 2 to 3 hours according to size, in salted water. Drain and cool and remove the skin. Slice the beetroot very thinly and put it into a lined pan in which has been melted half an ounce of butter. Re-heat carefully so as not to smash the beetroot and then add 1 tablespoonful of vinegar and a dust of pepper. Serve very hot. It is a good plan to re-heat in a French casserole which can be sent straight to table and will retain the heat longer than a vegetable dish.

BOSTON BAKED BEANS. (109)

1 pint small Haricot Beans.	6 ozs. Fat Bacon or Salt Pork.
1 tablespoonful Molasses.	1 tablespoonful Sugar.
1 cupful Boiling Water.	

Pick over the beans, wash well and leave to soak overnight. Drain well and put on to cook with fresh water to cover. Let them heat slowly and cook till skins will burst. In America it is quite usual to test beans by taking a few on the end of a spoon and blowing upon them to see if the skins will burst. The beans tested in this way must, of course, be thrown away. Drain the beans. Have a thick slice of fat bacon or salt pork and from the rind end cut a slice quarter of an inch thick and lay it on the bottom of a deep earthenware pot. Put in the beans and then the bacon amongst them cut in inch blocks. Mix the molasses, sugar, salt and pepper and pour the boiling water into them. Mix well and add to the pot. Add sufficient boiling water after that to come to the top of the beans, then put on a close fitting lid and bake slowly for eight hours.

The quantity of salt depends upon the kind used and also upon the bacon or salt pork. Some people think that the beans are more easily digested if a teaspoonful of mustard is mixed with the seasonings.

BRUSSELS SPROUTS WITH ONION.   (110)

1 lb. Brussels Sprouts.	$\frac{1}{2}$ oz. Butter.
1 large Spanish Onion.	Salt and Pepper.

Scald, dry and grate the onion and fry slowly in the butter till golden brown. Add the sprouts which should be boiled till quite tender and very thoroughly drained. Toss together and serve very hot.

CAROTTES LYONNAISE.   (111)

In the South of France one is often struck by the flavour and appearance of the young carrots which are so frequently served, and a few words of appreciation called forth an invitation from the cook to see how they were prepared. It was an agreeable surprise to find that the method employed was at once more simple and expeditious than the one most generally taught in this country.

You take a bunch of young carrots and hold it under the water tap to free from grit. Cut off the leaves and plunge the carrots into salted boiling water and boil till tender. Drain off the water and slip off the skins as you would the skin of the beetroot. Cut off the ends and toss in a casserole in which some fresh butter has been melted. When thoroughly hot serve with finely chopped parsley sprinkled over.

CAULIFLOWER AND TOMATO SAUCE. (112)

1 Cauliflower.	½ pint Light Stock.
1 oz. Flour.	4 Tomatoes.
1 Rasher Fat Bacon.	½ teaspoonful Sugar.
1 Carrot (small).	2 tablespoonsful Milk.
1 Onion (small).	Salt and Pepper.

Fry bacon, onion and sugar together, add flour and cook for a few seconds. Add sliced tomatoes, mix well and allow to reduce for 5 minutes. Let all simmer slowly for one hour. Strain, re-heat, and before serving add the milk and season. Break the cauliflower into half a dozen pieces, remove the hard stalk at the end and boil till tender in salted water. Drain well, dish up, and pour the tomato sauce over. If tinned tomatoes are used the liquor can be substituted for the stock. This dish is very good served in a pie-dish with minced corned beef at the bottom and a liberal dusting of breadcrumbs and pats of margarine on top.

CELERY CUTLETS.   (113)

1 teacupful cooked Celery.	1 yoke of Egg.
1 oz. Butter.	$\frac{1}{2}$ oz. Grated Cheese.
1 oz. Flour.	Salt, Pepper and Cayenne.
1 gill White Stock or Milk.	Egg and Breadcrumbs.

Drain the celery very thoroughly and chop it. Melt the butter in a saucepan, add the flour and then thin down with the stock. Stir vigorously and let it cook till the mixture comes away from the sides of the pan into a ball. Take it from the fire and let it cool a little then add the celery, cheese, yolk of egg and seasoning and mix well. Lay on a plate to cool then form into small cutlets. Flour, dip in egg and breadcrumbs and fry in deep fat till golden brown.

GREEN CORN.   (114)

Many people avoid this vegetable because their cooks don't know how to cook it, but it is really very simple.

The husks should be removed, all except the inner layer, which must be turned back to remove the " silk " and any bad grains from the corn. Fold back again and tie at the top and cook in plenty of salted boiling water from 15 to 25 minutes, according to size of cob. Untie and serve very hot on a napkin with salt butter melted and handed separately.

CORN FRITTERS.   (115)

This American dish is excellent served with cold meat at lunch or with tomato sauce as a supper dish.

1 tin Corn.	4 tablespoonsful of Flour.
2 Eggs.	2 tablespoonsful Chopped
Salt and Pepper.	Parsley.

Turn the corn into a colander and drain well. Beat the eggs in a basin and add the corn. Mix in the flour and parsley, and season well. Fry dessert spoonsful of the mixture in a deep pan of smoking fat and drain on kitchen paper. Heat up the fat after each panful is finished, otherwise the fritters will be greasy. Pile up and serve plain or with sauce.

CURLY GREENS. (116)

This admirable winter vegetable is much improved by the addition of a piece of mutton fat to the water in which it is boiled. When fresh and tender it is useful when spinach is not to be had. If well drained and chopped very fine it can be used as a bed for poached eggs, bacon, etc., for luncheon dishes.

DRESSED FRENCH BEANS. (117)

1 lb. French Beans.	Pinch of Nutmeg.
1 oz. Butter.	1 dessertspoonful Chopped
1 teaspoonful Lemon Juice.	Parsley.
Salt and Pepper.	4 Rashers Bacon.

Pick and string beans and cut each into three strips. Wash well and put on in salted boiling water and boil fast without a lid until tender, which should be about 20 minutes. Young beans will take less and old probably more. Drain very well.

Melt butter in stewpan, add the seasoning and toss beans in it till quite hot. Dish in a neat mound and garnish with rolls of bacon.

The bacon should be cut thin and each rasher cut in two across, rolled up and stuck on a skewer and cooked for five minutes in the oven.

LEEKS AU GRATIN. (118)

½ doz. good sized Leeks. | 1½ ozs. Grated Cheese.
1½ gills White Sauce. |

Wash and trim the leeks carefully. Cut down the middle and leave in plenty of cold water for an hour. Tie together with a string and cook in salted boiling water till tender. Untie then drain thoroughly and cut in 3 inch lengths and lay on a greased fireproof baking dish.

Make the sauce and season it well, add half the cheese and pour over the leeks. Cover with the remainder of the cheese and bake in a good oven for 15 or 20 minutes.

BAKED MUSHROOMS. (119)

One of the most delicious ways of serving mushrooms is at the same time one of the simplest. Peel and trim the mushrooms and lay on a greased baking sheet. Cover with greased paper and bake in a good oven till done, which will be roughly about 15 minutes, but depends on mushrooms and heat of oven.

For those who like the flavour of bacon, use bacon fat instead of butter for greasing and serve on hot toast.

PARSNIPS À LA CRÈME. (120)

4 or 6 Parsnips. | 1½ gills White Sauce.
Salt. | Lemon Juice.
½ oz. Butter. | Chopped Parsley.

Peel and wash 4 or 6 parsnips, according to size, and cut into large dice. Put into salted boiling water and add a squeeze of lemon juice. Cook till tender and drain well. Melt the butter in a saucepan, add the parsnips and toss in it. Add the white sauce, which should be nicely seasoned, and when it comes to the boil dish at once in a heap and sprinkle finely chopped parsley over.

PARSNIP PURÉE. (121)

4 Parsnips.	1 tablespoonful Cream.
1 oz. Butter.	Salt and Pepper.

Wash and scrape the parsnips and cut into pieces. Cook till tender in salted boiling water—they will take about an hour. Drain and pass through a fine sieve.

Melt the butter in the pan and re-heat the purée in it. Add seasonings and then the cream and make very thoroughly hot before using.

GREEN PEA PURÉE. (122)

1 package Dried Green Peas.	2 Cloves.
1 Onion.	1 teaspoonful Sugar.
1 oz. Butter.	Salt and Pepper.
Stock.	Sprig of Mint or Dried Mint.

Soak the peas according to directions given on the package. Put on in cold water and when it boils add the onion stuck with cloves, and the mint and sugar. When tender pass through a fine sieve and return to the pan with the butter and re-heat. Add a little stock or milk if too dry and season well with salt and pepper. Form into a neat border.

Like all the pulses, peas should not have salt added to them till they are quite cooked, as it hardens the outer fibre and prevents them becoming as soft as they ought to be.

PEAS À LA FRANÇAISE. (123)

1 pint young Peas.	1 large Lettuce.
3 green Onions.	1 slice Raw Ham.
4 leaves Mint.	2 Cloves.
Salt and Pepper.	

Melt butter in an earthenware or white lined pan and cook the onions, very thinly sliced, for a few minutes. Add the bacon in strips, the lettuce in shreds, mint and peas. Season and cook gently in their own juice with a good fitting lid on saucepan for about three-quarters of an hour.

This dish is not suitable for old peas.

POMMES DE TERRE SOUFFLÉES. (124)

Peel some small, even-sized Dutch potatoes and cut them in thin slices. Soak in cold water for an hour. Dry well and fry in hot but not smoking fat. When they begin to float, drain them and heat up the fat till it smokes. Return potatoes to this and they will then puff out and brown. Drain and sprinkle with salt and serve very hot.

BLACK POTATOES. (125)

When potatoes are old they often become black when they are boiled. It is an excellent plan to add 1 teaspoonful white vinegar to the pint of water ten minutes before draining the potatoes. This improves the appearance very much and does not spoil the flavour at all. Lemon juice can be substituted for vinegar if preferred.

CREAMY POTATOES. (126)

To improve the flavour and appearance of mashed potatoes add a nut of butter and a little hot milk and beat over the fire with a strong fork till light and creamy. Serve at once with finely chopped parsley sprinkled on top.

HARD POTATOES. (127)

Baked potatoes are often served with very hard outside skins, due to long baking in the oven. This can be avoided by parboiling them for 15 minutes in salted water, drying them, and, before putting into the oven, ruffling the outside with a short pronged fork. When baked they will then have a rough, attractive appearance and be much more easily digested.

SAVOURY POTATOES. (128)

This dish is excellent served with cold meat of any sort and it can be heated up again like a milk pudding, or eaten cold. It makes a useful lunch or supper vegetable.

6 Potatoes.	¾ pint Milk.
1 Onion.	Salt and Pepper.

Grease a pie-dish and put in a layer of thinly sliced raw potato. Grate a little onion over the potato and season it. Fill the pie-dish ¾ full in this manner and then pour the milk over. Put in a fairly hot oven and bake for an hour and a half. It should be soft and creamy when it is cooked properly and not at all dry.

STOVED POTATOES.   (129)

This is a very old way of cooking new potatoes and they are particularly good eaten with cold meat for lunch.

1¼ lbs. New Potatoes.	Salt and Pepper.
6 or 8 Syboes.	Roast Beef Dripping.

Scrape potatoes, wash syboes and cut up in slices, using quite a good bit of the green as well as the white part. Put all into pan, add salt, cover with boiling water and cook till potatoes just begin to show signs of softening. Drain carefully, to keep in as much as possible of the syboe, and add a piece of good brown roast beef dripping about the size of a large walnut and a good shake of black pepper. Put on lid and cook till soft. Shake up well and serve very hot.

POTATO AND ONION FRITTERS.   (130)

¾ lb. Potatoes.	4 ozs. Flour.
6 ozs. Spanish Onion.	1 Egg.
½ teaspoonful Royal Baking Powder.	Salt and Pepper.

Peel the potatoes and onion and grate them both into a basin. Sieve the flour, salt and pepper into a basin. Make a well in the centre and drop in the egg. Beat it into the flour and by degrees add a little of the onion mixture and beat it all very well indeed till the air bells rise. Add remainder of the potato and onion.

Have a pan of deep fat ready and, just before beginning to fry the fritters, add the baking powder and mix well in.

Drop the mixture off the point of a dessertspoon and fry a nice brown. Drain on paper and serve as hot as possible garnished with fried parsley.

Do not fry too many fritters at a time as this cools the fat too much and the fritters will be greasy. If the fat is re-heated between each lot these fritters will be found exceedingly crisp and savoury.

TOMATOES AU GRATIN. (131)

6 Tomatoes.	3 tablespoonsful Grated Cheese.
1 tablespoonful Butter.	3 tablespoonsful Breadcrumbs.
Salt and Pepper.	

Put the tomatoes into boiling water for a minute, and then remove the skins. Butter a fireproof gratin dish ; mix the breadcrumbs and cheese together and dust the bottom of the dish with them. Cover with a layer of sliced tomatoes, season well and repeat till all is used up.

Cover over with breadcrumbs and cheese and put pats of butter on top. Bake in a good oven for half an hour when it should be soft and nicely browned.

STUFFED TOMATOES. (132)

6 Tomatoes.	2 Lettuce.
1 cupful Walnuts.	Cream Dressing.
1 cupful Peas.	Salt and Pepper.

Choose round good sized tomatoes and scoop out the centres. Cook young peas with a small teaspoonful of sugar and a sprig of mint till tender, drain well and cool. Break up the walnuts roughly. Wash and dry the lettuce carefully and use only the crisp inside leaves. Mix the peas and walnuts together with sufficient cream dressing to moisten them and fill the tomatoes with the mixture. Dish up neatly with crisp lettuce hearts round each. If possible lay on ice for an hour before serving.

˙ASPARAGUS SALAD.   (133)

1 tin Asparagus.	Cream Dressing.
Rings of Carrot.	Lettuce.

Drain the asparagus from the liquor in the tin.   Stamp
out rings about ¼ of an inch wide from a parboiled carrot,
lay 3 or 4 stalks of asparagus in each and serve on a bed of
crisp lettuce.   Hand cream dressing separately.

BANANA SALAD.   (134)

Bananas.	Lettuce.
1oz. Walnuts (shelled).	Cream Mayonnaise Dressing.

This salad should not be prepared for any length of
time before it is to be served as the banana is apt to
become brown from exposure to the air.

Blanch and peel the walnuts and chop roughly.   Peel
and scrape the banana and cut in ½ inch slices.   Wash and
dry very thoroughly some crisp leaves of a cabbage
lettuce.   Serve the bananas and walnuts in heaps upon
these leaves and pour over each a little cream dressing
mixed with lemon in place of vinegar.   Serve as cold as
possible.

COPLEY-PLAZA SALAD.   (135)

Celery.	Apple.
Orange.	Grape Fruit.

This delicious salad is composed of equal quantities of
crisp celery and apple, cut up small, and orange and grape
fruit, scooped out with a teaspoon, and all mixed together.
It is served on crisp lettuce leaves on individual glass
plates with a rather sweet cream dressing.

. CREAM CHEESE WALNUT SALAD. (136)

1 Cream Cheese.	Chopped Pistachio Nuts.
1 tablespoonful Cream.	Curled Celery.
Halved Walnuts.	Lettuce.
French Dressing.	Pepper and Salt.

Wash and scrape the celery and with a sharp knife cut it down in fine strips almost to the foot of stalk. Put in cold water for an hour or more till it curls. Wash and dry the lettuce carefully. Break up the cheese with a fork and add salt and pepper and mix well with the cream to a nice consistency. Form into balls and press a half walnut on each side then dip in finely chopped pistachio nuts. Arrange the lettuce on a glass dish with alternate heaps of walnuts and curled celery. Just before serving springle over a dressing made of 1 tablespoonful vinegar and 2 tablespoonsful salad oil, beaten together with salt and pepper.

DANISH SALAD. (137)

3 Tomatoes.	1 Apple.
1 head Celery.	1 oz. Walnuts.
Finely Chopped Parsley.	Cream Dressing.

Clean the celery and reject all but the very whitest parts Cut it in 3 inch lengths and shred down rather thicker than a large match. Let it lie in very cold salted water for a couple of hours, or longer, till it curls.

Dip the tomatoes separately in absolutely boiling water and remove the skins. Let them cool, then slice and make a neat border round a rather flat salad dish. Peel and core a well flavoured dessert apple and cut in large dice. Make a ring of the apple inside the tomatoes and fill the centre with the curled celery which should be well dried

F

and piled high. Blanch the walnuts, break in two and sprinkle over. Dust some very dry and finely chopped parsley over all and put a few tiny stems of celery leaves standing straight up in the centre. Serve with cream dressing mixed with lemon juice in place of vinegar.

INDIAN SALAD.   (138)

1 tin Curried Prawns.	Mustard and Cress.
2 hard boiled Eggs.	1 teaspoonful Indian Chutney.
1 large Lettuce.	1 dessertspoonful Wine Vinegar.
1 glass Claret.	

Choose a large cabbage lettuce, wash and dry it well, also the mustard and cress. Tear up the lettuce and mix all green things together. Heap up on a flat dish and arrange the eggs round, cut in four lengthways. Arrange the prawns round the outside and, just before serving, sprinkle with salt and make a dressing of the claret, vinegar and chutney and pour it over. Serve with brown bread and butter.

JUTLAND SALAD.   (139)

1 teacupful Macaroni (cooked).	1 gill Cream.
1 teacupful Flaked Fish (cooked).	1 tablespoonful Tarragon Vinegar.
3 ozs. Grated Horse Radish.	Chopped Tarragon.
Salt and Pepper.	Lettuce.
½ teaspoonful Made Mustard.	

Have the macaroni well drained and cut in ½ inch lengths and mix it with the flaked fish. Whip the cream and add the grated radish and seasonings and then stir in the vinegar. Mix the macaroni and fish very lightly in this dressing with a couple of forks and arrange in a salad bowl surrounded by crisp hearts of lettuce and sprinkle a little finely chopped tarragon over.

ORANGE SALAD.　　(140)

2 Sweet Oranges.	A few slices Cold Potato.
1 small Lettuce.	Cream Dressing.

Cut the oranges across in half and with the handle of a teaspoon cut the orange clean out of the skin. Cut the orange into neat pieces and arrange daintily in the empty orange skins with the potato and some fresh tufts of lettuce. Pour over a few drops of cream dressing and serve very cold on individual plates.

It is best not to prepare oranges too long before they are wanted.

A WINTER SALAD.　　(141)

Celery.	Cheese Cream Dressing.
Potatoes.	Chopped Parsley or Mustard and
Beetroot.	Cress.

Cut equal quantities of crisp celery, cold boiled potato and beetroot into neat blocks.

Make a mound of the potato in the centre of the salad dish and dust it liberally with either finely chopped parsley or picked mustard and cress. Then make a ring of celery and outside that a ring of beetroot. For a gill of dressing add a heaped dessertspoonful of grated and finely sieved cheese to the usual hard boiled yolk of egg and blend it very well before adding to other ingredients.

SAUCES AND SALAD DRESSINGS.

In many households far too little attention is paid to the preparation of sauces. They are frequently left over till the last minute and hurriedly prepared, with results which are far from satisfactory.

A single-handed cook should make her sauces beforehand and turn them into jam pots which will keep them in excellent condition if placed in a stewpan of boiling water to keep hot. The jam pots should of course be covered.

APPLE SAUCE. (142)

1 lb. Apples, or	$\frac{1}{2}$ oz. Butter.
$\frac{1}{2}$ lb. Apple Rings.	1 oz. Sugar.
1 gill Water.	

Peel, core and slice apples and put in a pan with butter and sugar and stew till soft. Beat smooth with wooden spoon and serve separately. If dried apples are used soak in $\frac{1}{2}$ pint water, after washing well, and finish in the same way.

BREAD SAUCE. (143)

$\frac{1}{2}$ pint Milk.	1 oz. Butter.
1 small Onion.	$\frac{1}{4}$ Blade of Mace.
1 gill Breadcrumbs.	6 White Peppercorns.
Salt.	

Put onion, cut in two and scalded, with the mace and peppercorns into a lined pan and let them infuse in the milk for half an hour. Strain and return to the pan with the butter and freshly sieved breadcrumbs. Season and cook gently till the breadcrumbs have absorbed the milk. Two tablespoonsful of cream greatly improve this sauce.

BROWN SAUCE PIQUANTE. (144)

1½ ozs. Butter.	½ a Carrot.
1 oz. Flour.	1 Rasher Lean Bacon.
Small Onion.	½ pint Brown Stock.
1 Tomato.	½ dozen Peppercorns.
Small Bunch Herbs.	Salt.
1 Gherkin, chopped.	1 teaspoonful Capers.
1 dessertspoonful Vinegar.	1 teaspoonful chopped Parsley.

Slice carrot and onion and fry with the bacon in the butter for 5 minutes. Add the flour and cook slowly till golden brown, being careful not to let it stick. Add the tomato cut up, and then the stock by degrees. When it boils add the peppercorns and salt with the herbs. Simmer all gently for 40 minutes, then pass through a hair sieve. Add the capers, gherkin, parsley and vinegar and boil up once.

VEGETARIAN BROWN SAUCE. (145)

This is a very useful and economical sauce which can take the place of gravy in many instances and appeals especially to those who are often, like the immortal Mrs. Todgers, at their wits' end to provide sufficient gravy " which a whole animal, not to speak of a j'int wouldn't do."

½ pint Water.	1 small Onion.
½ oz. Flour.	1 teaspoonful Marmite.
½ oz. Butter.	Pepper.

Slice onion thinly and fry in the butter. Add the flour and brown it, then the marmite. Thin down with the water, which should be boiling. Season and cook for half an hour. Strain into gravy boat.

The addition of a few pieces of celery, or a tomato makes variety.

CELERY SAUCE FOR BOILED TURKEY. (146)

1½ ozs. Flour.	Small Head of Celery.
1½ ozs. Butter.	White Stock and Milk.
Salt and Pepper.	

Thoroughly clean the celery and use only the white parts. Cut it in thin slices and stew in delicately flavoured stock and milk in equal proportions till tender. Pass through a hair sieve. Melt the butter in a saucepan, add the flour and thin down with about a pint of the liquor the celery was cooked in. Let it boil for 10 minutes then add the celery pulp and bring to boiling point again. Season and pour over the turkey.

CURRY SAUCE. (147)

1 small Onion.	1 teaspoonful Curry Powder.
1 oz. Margarine.	1 dessertspoonful Cocoanut.
½ an Apple.	½ oz. Flour.
½ pint Light Stock.	Lemon Juice and Salt.

Fry the onion, curry powder and apple in the margarine, add the flour and cocoanut. Thin down with the stock and season. Let it simmer for three-quarters of an hour and strain it. Before serving add a dash of lemon juice, and, if possible, 2 tablespoonsful of cream.

GOOSEBERRY SAUCE. (148)

½ pint Green Gooseberries.	1 teaspoonful Sugar.
½ pint melted Butter Sauce.	1 tablespoonful Water.

Top and tail the berries and stew in water and sugar till soft. Pass through a sieve and add to the sauce. Re-heat and serve. Allow ½ oz. butter and same of flour to ½ pint water for the melted butter, and season to taste.

CURRANT MINT SAUCE. (149)

For this delicious accompaniment to roast mutton take one half pound pot of red currant jelly and break it up lightly with a silver knife, but do not beat it. Add 1½ tablespoonsful very finely chopped fresh mint and mix lightly. Remove all the pith from the rind of a smooth skinned orange, shred it very finely and sprinkle over. Serve in a glass dish.

MINT SAUCE. (150)

With the advent of lamb comes mint sauce, and very badly made it often is. The usual method of chopping the mint does not extract from it the essential oil of the mint, nor does it make a blend of the ingredients. The sauce made in the following way may not look quite so nice, but with improved flavour that may be overlooked.

Take a handful of mint and strip off the fresh leaves. Put into a mortar with 2 tablespoons of coarse granulated sugar and pound to a pulp. Add 2 tablespoonsful of boiling water and mix well, then add 2 tablespoonsful vinegar. Let it stand for an hour and serve.

If a mortar is not available, a small potato masher and strong bowl answer very well.

WALNUT GRAVY. (151)

This makes a very nourishing sauce which is useful for serving with made-up dishes.

2 ozs. Ground Walnuts.	1 teaspoonful Grated Onion.
1 oz. Butter.	½ pint Brown Stock.
¾ oz. Flour.	Salt and Pepper.
1 Tomato.	

Brown walnuts, onions and flour slowly in the butter. Add the tomato in slices and then by degrees the brown stock. Simmer for 20 minutes. Strain, season and serve.

COLD DUTCH SAUCE.   (152)

This is an excellent recipe.   It is useful for serving with all manner of cold dishes, and is both economical and quickly made.

3 level teaspoonsful Flour.	1½ ozs. Butter.
6 tablespoonsful Water.	1 Yolk of Egg.
1½ tablespoonsful Vinegar.	Salt and Pepper.
1 tablespoonful Cucumber.	

Melt butter in pan, add flour and mix.   Thin down with water and vinegar mixed.   Season and cook slowly for 10 minutes.   Remove from fire, cool very slightly, add the yolk of egg, beat well, and stir in one direction till it is almost cold.   When cold add the cucumber in strips about ½ an inch long, and about the breadth of a match.   Serve very cold.

SALAD DRESSING THAT WILL KEEP. (153)

This dressing is much appreciated by those who object to the flavour of salad oil.   It should be poured into a wide necked bottle and, if it is well corked, it will keep for weeks.

2 hard boiled yolks of Eggs.	3 teaspoonsful Castor Sugar.
1 teaspoonful Salt.	1 gill Cream.
1 teaspoonful made Mustard.	Vinegar and Pepper.

Boil the eggs for 20 minutes and put at once into cold water.   When cool remove the yolks and pass through a fine sieve.   Add the sugar, salt, pepper and mix.   Make into a perfectly smooth paste with the cream adding only a little at a time.   Then add the made mustard and thin down with about 2 tablespoonsful of vinegar, which should be added by degrees and well mixed in.   The question of the amount of vinegar depends on the quality of the vinegar used and the individual taste.

POTATO MAYONNAISE.   (154)

This is a very inexpensive dressing and very easily prepared.

1 small cooked Potato.	2 tablespoonsful Vinegar.
1 teaspoonful Made Mustard.	¾ of a gill Olive Oil.
1 teaspoonful Salt.	½ teaspoonful Castor Sugar.
Pinch of Pepper.	

Mash the potato, add the seasonings and 1 tablespoonful vinegar. Pass through a fine sieve. Add the oil slowly, beating well all the while, and lastly the remainder of the vinegar. The dressing should be sufficiently thick to coat the back of the wooden spoon it is mixed with.

APRICOT SAUCE.   (155)

2 tablespoonsful Apricot Jam.	1 oz. Sugar.
1 gill Water.	1 teaspoonful Potato Flour.
Juice of ¼ of a Lemon.	

Break the potato flour (or cornflour if more convenient) with a spoonful of water. Put jam, sugar, water and lemon juice on to boil. Skim well and add the potato flour. Boil for 5 minutes and strain round the pudding.

BRANDY SAUCE.   (156)

1 oz. Butter.	1 glass Brandy.
½ oz. Flour.	1½ gills Water.
¾ oz. Sugar.	

Melt butter in a saucepan and add flour. Thin down with the water and cook for 10 minutes. Add the sugar and, just before sending to table, stir in the brandy.

HARD SAUCE. (157)

2 ozs. Butter.   Essence of Almonds.
2 ozs. Castor Sugar.

Beat butter and sugar till very light and creamy and
flavour with almond or any essence which may be
preferred. Where expense need not be considered,
substitute ½ glass of sherry for flavouring essence.

Pile roughly on a glass dish and hand with the pudding.

CRANBERRY HARD SAUCE. (158)

2 ozs. Butter.   Cranberry Juice.
4 ozs. Sugar.

Cream the butter, and add the sugar by degrees. Add
sufficient strained cranberry juice to colour nicely. Pile
on a glass dish, or pipe through a large rose pipe on to a
dish, and decorate with leaves of candied angelica. Serve
hard with the pudding.

NUT SAUCE. (159)

4 ozs. Butter.   2 tablespoonsful Chopped
4 ozs. Castor Sugar.   Almonds.
                         2 tablespoonsful Sherry.

Cream butter with a fork till very light, add the sugar
by degrees and continue creaming. Mix in the almonds
and by degrees the sherry, beating it well into the mixture.
Pile up roughly on a crystal dish and hand with the
pudding.

PUDDINGS.

APPLE PUDDING. (160)

Many people who are very busy grudge the time taken up in making an apple dumpling. There is a basin, board and rolling pin to wash before the pudding is cooked at all. Now this recipe is given for such as those. It doesn't pretend to be any better than the old apple dumpling, but it does save work and is very good indeed.

½ lb. Flour.	4 good-sized Apples.
¼ lb. Margarine.	½ teaspoonful Borwick's Baking
Sugar.	Powder.
Cold Water.	Pinch of Salt.

Peel and core the apples and cut in chunks the size of a small walnut. Lay on a piece of clean paper and strew them with sugar.

Sift the flour, salt and baking powder into the basin the pudding is to be cooked in. Cut up the margarine in the flour with a knife. Then rub it in till like breadcrumbs. With the knife mix to a soft dough with the cold water—considerably softer than for suet pastry. Turn the apples and sugar into this and mix very well. Cover with a greased paper and steam for 2 to 2½ hours. Remove the paper and serve with a napkin folded round.

Hard sauce is very delicious with apple pudding.

APRICOT FRITTERS.   (161)

½ tin Apricots.	1 oz. Butter.
4 ozs. Flour.	1 Egg.
1 gill Apricot Juice.	Pinch of Salt.
Castor Sugar.	

Drain the apricots in a colander.   Sieve flour and salt into a basin.   Melt margarine and slightly heat the juice —it should be about tepid.   Add yolk of egg to flour, then butter and some juice and beat very well till free from lumps.   Thin down with remainder of juice and let it stand 1 hour.   Before using fold in the stiffly beaten white of egg.   Dip the apricots in this batter and fry a golden brown in deep fat.   Drain on paper, dish up and dredge with castor sugar.

APRICOT PUDDING.   (162)

2 ozs. Butter.	Pinch of Salt.
1 oz. Sugar.	5 ozs. Flour.
1 teaspoonful Baking Powder.	1 Egg.
1 tablespoonful Apricot Jam.	

Sift the flour, baking powder and salt.   Cream butter and sugar till very light. Drop in the yolk of the egg and a very little flour and beat well.   Add the jam and remaining flour, mix well and last of all fold in the stiffly beaten white of egg.   Steam for 1½ hours.   Turn out and serve with apricot sauce round.

BARONESS PUDDING.   (163)

½ lb. Flour.	6 ozs. Suet.
½ lb. Seeded Raisins.	½ pint Milk.
Pinch of Salt.	

Shred and chop the suet very finely indeed and sieve the flour.   Cut the raisins in half and mix all dry things well together.   Make into a nice soft dough with the milk but do not add all of it at once as sometimes less may do—it depends upon the flour. It should not be too soft or the fruit will not be well mixed through the pudding. Boil in a cloth for 4½ hours or in a basin for 5. Turn out and serve with castor sugar.

This is an excellent pudding.

CHOCOLATE PUDDING. (164)

4 ozs. Cadbury's Mexican Chocolate.	½ pint Milk. 3 Eggs.
3 ozs. Castor Sugar.	½ teaspoonful Essence of
4 ozs. Sponge Cake.	Vanilla.

Crumb the sponge cake and put it with the chocolate (grated) and milk into a saucepan and boil till the mixture leaves the sides of the pan quite clean, taking care that it does not stick to the pan.

Take off the fire and add the sugar and when it has cooled a little add the yolks of the eggs. Then add the essence of vanilla and last of all fold in the stiffly beaten whites of eggs. Turn into a well greased mould and steam gently for 1½ hours. Turn out and serve with wine sauce or whipped cream sweetened and flavoured with vanilla.

CURATE PUDDING. (165)

2 Eggs.	Weight of 2 Eggs in each—
2 teaspoonsful Lemon Peel.	Flour, Butter and Sugar.
½ teaspoonful Baking Powder.	

Beat the butter and sugar till white and very light. Sieve the flour, add the eggs singly with a spoonful of flour. Beat each one very well. Shred the lemon peel finely and add it and the baking powder with the last of the flour.

Butter a mould and dust it out with equal quantities of flour and castor sugar mixed together. Bake the pudding in this for about ¾ of an hour. Turn out and serve with custard sauce flavoured with lemon rind.

FRENCH PANCAKES.   (166)

2 ozs. Butter.	2 Eggs.
2 ozs. Rice Flour.	1½ gills Warm Milk.
2 ozs. Sugar.	Jam and Sugar.

Grease some good sized flat patty pans and dust with flour.   Cream butter and sugar, add flour and eggs singly, and beat very well.   Add warm milk by degrees—rather slowly.   Bake in patty tins in a hot oven for 7 to 10 minutes.   Turn on to paper dredged with castor sugar. Put hot jam on every second one and sandwich together. Serve very hot.

FIG PUDDING.   (167)

Some people find the usual fig pudding, made with suet and flour, rather heavy and for those this recipe may be useful ; it makes a light and nourishing pudding.

1 breakfastcupful Diced Bread.	1 tablespoonful Butter.
1½ breakfastcupsful Milk.	8 or 9 Figs.
2 Eggs, fresh or dried.	Pinch of Grated Lemon Rind.
1 tablespoonful Sugar.	

Stew the figs in an earthenware dish till tender.   Drain well and chop them.   Cut the bread in dice.   Heat the milk, butter and sugar and pour over the bread.   Let it stand for a few minutes then add the figs and lemon rind. Last of all add the eggs well beaten.   Turn into a greased basin and steam for 2½ hours.   Serve with cream.

This pudding can be varied with prunes, raisins, china ginger, etc., and served with various sauces to suit the fruit used.

HASTY PUDDING. (168

1 pint Milk.	Demerara Sugar.
3 ozs. Flour.	½ oz. Fresh Butter.
Salt.	

Break the flour to a perfectly smooth paste with a little of the milk, and put the rest on to boil. When it boils add the flour and a good pinch of salt. Let it boil for ten minutes, stirring well. Pour into hot pie dish and sprinkle well with demerara sugar, and put the fresh butter in pats on the top. Serve at once and hand demerera sugar with it. Unless the milk is absolutely boiling when the flour is added the flavour of the pudding will be spoiled.

PLUM PUDDING. (169)

½ lb. Raisins.	¼ lb. Brown Sugar.
½ lb. Currants.	½ lb. Suet.
½ lb. Breadcrumbs.	2 ozs. Flour.
1 large Apple.	1 tablespoonful Grated Carrot.
½ teaspoonful Ground Ginger.	¼ Nutmeg (grated).
½ teaspoonful Ground Cinnamon.	½ oz. Orange Peel.
½ teaspoonful Salt.	½ oz. Lemon Peel.
1 teaspoonful Gtd. Lemon Rind.	½ oz. Citron Peel.
½ glass Brandy.	1 glass Stout.
½ teacupful Milk.	2 Eggs.

Prepare the fruit. Shred the suet and peel and chop the apple finely. Sieve flour and breadcrumbs. Grate nutmeg, carrot and lemon rind and mix all well together with the sugar and spices. Beat the eggs well and add with the milk to the mixture. Lastly add the brandy and stout. Put into greased pudding basins, cover with a cloth which has been greased and floured and boil for at least 6 hours the first day. Boil for at least an hour before serving. Allow room for the puddings to swell in the basins and be careful to see that the water does not stop boiling while the pudding is in it.

PLAIN PLUM PUDDING. (170)

2 ozs. Flour.	1 oz. Peel.
2 ozs. Breadcrumbs.	2 ozs. Sugar.
4 ozs. Suet.	1 Egg.
4 ozs. Currants.	½ teaspoonful Mixed Spice.
2 ozs. Sultanas.	1 gill Milk.
2 ozs. Raisins.	2 ozs. Apple.

Clean and pick over the sultanas and currants and stone the raisins. Shred the peel and suet and mince the apple. Sieve the flour and breadcrumbs and mix all the dry ingredients together. Beat the egg well and mix with the milk. Make into a soft dough and boil for six hours the first day.

POTATO AND LEMON CUSTARD. (171)

½ lb. Peeled Potatoes.	1½ ozs. Butter.
1 gill Milk.	2 tablespoonsful Sugar.
1 Egg.	Rind and juice of 1 Lemon.

Boil and sieve the potatoes. Add the butter, lemon rind and juice and the sugar. Beat together till very smooth. Add the yolk of egg and then the milk. Last of all the white of egg, very stiffly beaten, should be folded in. Bake in a well greased pie-dish for about 40 minutes.

RHUBARB CHARLOTTE. (172)

Rhubarb.	Canton Ginger.
Butter.	Bread.
Sugar.	

Grease a pie-dish well with butter and line it closely and neatly with slices of thin bread and butter.

Wipe the rhubarb and cut it down quite small, also cut the ginger in small pieces. Mix all with brown sugar and fill up the pie dish with it. Cover with a good layer of fresh breadcrumbs and dot little pieces of butter over the top. Bake for an hour and a half in a steady oven. Turn out and serve with cream or hard sauce.

Allow 1 oz. of Canton ginger to each pound of rhubarb.

RICE AND CHOCOLATE SAUCE. (173)

This is an exceedingly economical pudding and is always much appreciated by the children.

¼ lb. Rice.	1 heaped tablespoonful Icing Sugar.
½ pint Water or Milk.	
2 heaped tablespoonsful Cadbury's Mexican Chocolate grated.	1 level tablespoonful Peterkin Corn Flour.
	½ teaspoonful Essence of Vanilla.

Wash well and cook the rice in a large panful of fast boiling water without a lid. As soon as it is done enough (which can be easily ascertained by pressing a grain between the finger and thumb), drain it and run plenty of cold water through it till free from starch. Dry it carefully in a rather cool oven, stirring with a fork to keep the grains perfectly free.

Pile up in a glass dish, and hand the sauce separately.

Mix the chocolate and sugar to a smooth paste with a little water. Add the rest of the liquid and stir till it boils. Cook 5 minutes. Break the cornflour in a little extra water and add to the chocolate. Stir till it boils and cook for another 5 minutes.

Add vanilla just before serving. Two teaspoonsful of brandy greatly improves this sauce, if for grown-ups.

G

SEVEN CUP PUDDING. (174)

This pudding is a great favourite with those who like a moderately plain fruit pudding. It keeps well and can be of the greatest use as a standby if prepared in quantities.

In one household the fruit for a double quantity is given out, when it is cleaned and stoned, the suet and buttermilk are ordered, and the puddings mixed up. The mixture is then divided into bowls to suit the size of the household. These are cooked in a large fish kettle and laid away in a dry place for emergencies. A piece of paper is tied over each to keep the dust out. With very little trouble a nice fruit pudding can be served at an hour's notice. These will keep good for several months, if they escape consumption.

The proportions are :—

1 breakfastcupful Flour.
1 breakfastcupful Currants.
1 breakfastcupful Sugar.
1 breakfastcupful Buttermilk.
1 teaspoonful Mixed Spice.
$\frac{1}{2}$ teaspoonful Cinnamon.
Pinch of Salt.
1 breakfastcupful Breadcrumbs.

1 breakfastcupful Suet.
1 breakfastcupful Muscatel Raisins.
2 Eggs
$\frac{1}{4}$ teaspoonful Ground Ginger.
$\frac{3}{4}$ teaspoonful Bi-Carb. of Soda.
$1\frac{1}{2}$ ozs. Mixed Peel.

Clean and pick the currants and stone the raisins. Shred the suet very finely and chop with a little of the flour. Sift the flour, soda and spices. Beat the eggs well. Mix dry ingredients together, then add eggs and buttermilk. Put into well greased basins, allowing room for puddings to swell, and steam 5 hours. To re-heat, steam 1 hour, or longer, if time permits. Serve with clear, custard or hard sauce.

SYRUP PUDDING.   (175)

Syrup is useful in so many ways in cooking that it should always be in the store cupboard.   Combined with good suet pastry it makes a capital cold weather pudding.

The recipe given below is for a steamed pudding but it is equally good as a roly poly either boiled or baked with margarine in place of suet for shortening.

PASTRY.—8 ozs. Flour.
4 ozs. Suet.

½ teaspoonful Baking Powder,
Cold Water and Salt.

FILLING.—1 teacupful Westburn Syrup.
¾ teacupful Breadcrumbs.

Grated Rind of 1 Lemon.
Juice of ½ Lemon.

Sieve the flour, baking powder and a pinch of salt. Shred and chop the suet very finely   The finer the suet is chopped the better the pudding will be.   Rub the suet into the flour, mix to a soft dough with cold water and roll out. Mix the syrup and breadcrumbs with the lemon rind and juice and put a little in the bottom of a well greased basin. Cut a ring of pastry and lay it over the syrup.   Continue with layers of pastry and syrup till all is used and have pastry on top   Allow room for pudding to swell, cover with a greased paper and steam for 3 hours·   Turn out and serve very hot.

BLAKEMORE PUDDING.   (176)

PASTRY.—4 ozs. Flour.
3 ozs. Peterkin Cornflour.
4 ozs. Butter.
1 oz. Castor Sugar.
Beaten yolk of Egg and Milk to bind.

FILLING.—1 Sponge Cake (Twopenny size).
3 tablespoonsful Raspberry Jam.
Grated rind and juice of small Lemon.

Make short crust pastry with first ingredients.   Cut it in two and roll out thin enough to cover a plate.   Lay in the filling, all well mixed together, and cover with pastry. Decorate with leaves of pastry and bake about 40 minutes in a good oven. Serve hot or cold with castor sugar dredged over.

CHESHIRE TART. (177)

¼ lb. Short Crust Pastry.	¾ pint Peterkin Custard.
4 Apples.	Nutmeg.
Marmalade.	

Line a pie dish half way down with the pastry and cut out stars from the scraps to ornament the edges.

Peel and core the apples, which should not weigh much more than 3 ozs. each, and lay in the pie dish. Fill the cores with marmalade or, if preferred, with apricot jam.

Make the custard according to directions on the package, sweeten well and pour over the apples. Grate some nutmeg over and bake slowly till the apples are soft, having the oven hotter for the first ten minutes to set the pastry.

Serve hot or cold.

DATE CUSTARD. (178)

This pudding has the advantage of requiring no sugar, and it is equally good hot or cold.

1½ pints Milk.	3 Eggs.
½ lb. Dates.	Nut of Butter.

Wash and stone the dates and stew gently in the milk till quite soft. Rub through a fine wire sieve. Beat the eggs well and strain into the mixture. Pour into a greased pie dish and bake till set in a moderate oven. This will take about 45 minutes. If baked too quickly it will be watery. When the custard is about half done it is a good plan to put the pie dish into a flat tin with cold water in it, if it shows signs of cooking too fast.

JAM TARTLETS. (179)

6 ozs. B.C.L. Lard.	½ teaspoonful Lemon Juice.
6 ozs. Flour.	Cold Water.
Pinch of Salt.	

Sieve flour and salt into a basin. Mix the lemon juice with about a teacupful of very cold water. Rub about ½ oz. of the lard into the flour and then mix with the water to a nice paste. Knead a little. Roll out and put all the remaining lard in a piece on the middle of the dough. Fold in three, seal the edges well, give pastry a half turn so that the ends come to the side. Roll out very thin, fold in three, seal edges and lay aside for half an hour in a very cold place. Give two more rolls and fold, seal after each and lay aside 15 minutes. Repeat till it has been rolled and folded 7 times.

Roll out as thin as half-a-crown. Stamp out in rounds and put into plain, rather deep, patty pans and lay aside for half an hour. Just before putting in the oven put a little round of paper in each and 1 teaspoonful of small dried beans to prevent the centres rising. Bake in a fairly hot oven. Remove beans and any damp dough from underneath.

Cool and fill with jam.

PRUNE MERINGUE. (180)

¾ lb. Prunes.	½ pint Water.
1½ ozs. Sugar.	2 Whites of Eggs.
Lemon Rind.	2 ozs. Castor Sugar.
1 inch Cinnamon Stick.	

Wash prunes and soak them overnight in the water. Put them into a casserole with the measured water, the cinnamon and lemon rind very thinly cut. Add the sugar and let them cook slowly with the lid on till perfectly tender. Drain and remove the stones, lemon rind and cinnamon. Break some of the stones, remove and blanch the kernels and add to the prunes.

Reduce the syrup by cooking without a lid till a nice consistency. The length of time required will depend upon how fast the prunes have cooked and their quality. Put the prunes into a white soufflé or pie dish, pour the syrup over and let them cool.

Beat up the whites of eggs very stiffly with a pinch of salt. By degrees add the castor sugar, pile roughly over the prunes, dust with castor sugar and put in a moderate oven till crisp. Serve hot or cold.

CHESTNUT VERMICELLI.   (181)

1 lb. Chestnuts.	Castor Sugar.
2 ozs. Chocolate.	Cream or Custard.

Put the chestnuts into cold water and cook till tender. They will take about half an hour after the water boils—if they are large. Remove the shells and skins and pass through a sieve. Melt the chocolate in the oven and sieve also. Mix very well together with a silver fork and add sugar to taste. Take a round glass dish and sieve the mixture right on to it, using a fairly coarse sieve. Serve with whipped cream, or cup custard, handed separately.

COFFEE JELLY.   (182)

1 pint Coffee.	1 oz. French Leaf Gelatine.
1 tablespoonful Sugar.	$\frac{1}{2}$ teaspoonful Essence of Vanilla.
1 gill Sweetened Cream.	Glacé Cherries.
Flavouring.	

Make the coffee, allowing 3 tablespoons to the pint of boiling water. Make rather more than the quantity required so as to get 1 pint coffee. Strain it through a very fine muslin into a porcelain-lined pan. Add the gelatine cut in small pieces and stir it over the fire till it dissolves. Add the sugar and vanilla essence. Strain into a basin and when almost cold pour into a border mould and leave till firm. Whip the cream, sweeten and flavour it to taste. Turn out the jelly, pile the cream in the centre and decorate with the cherries.

If a more inexpensive sweet is required set the jelly in an ordinary mould and serve with cup custard.

In cold weather use rather less gelatine or the jelly may be too stiff. Some cooks have a habit of not quite filling measures and this makes all the difference in the results obtained.

DANISH CREAM.   (183)

2½ ozs. Chocolate.	2 tablespoonsful Castor Sugar.
½ pint Cream.	5 ozs. Brown Bread.
Red Currant Jelly.	Candied Rose Leaves.

Grate the bread and sieve it, grate the chocolate (chocolate powder is not suitable) and mix with the bread-crumbs and the sugar. Whip the cream lightly and put a layer on the bottom of a glass dish. Cover with a layer of the chocolate mixture and cover this with a layer of red currant jelly, thinly spread. Add another layer of cream and then chocolate mixture and a thin layer of cream on top. If wanted for dinner prepare this early in the morning so that it will be moist, but if required for lunch, prepare it the night before. An hour before serving whip the remainder of the cream rather more and arrange roughly on the top with candied rose leaves, or, failing these, dabs of red currant jelly to give the Danish colours from which the pudding takes its name.

CUSTARD SPONGE. (184)

In these days when cream and eggs are so expensive, many people are unable to afford such delicacies as cream and sweet soufflés. To them this light pudding may be useful.

Make half a pint of cup custard but do not sweeten it. Lay it aside to cool.

Dissolve a pint packet of table jelly in ½ pint of boiling water in a good sized basin, and when it is cold, but not set, add the custard to it and beat both together with a " Dover " beater or wire whisk till a soft creamy sponge is formed. It will take about 10 to 15 minutes, and is more quickly done near an open door or window. Pour into a wet mould and turn out when set.

DORSET PUDDING. (185)

1 pint Buttermilk.	Juice of 1 Lemon.
¼ lb. Sugar.	Rind of ½ a Lemon.
5 sheets French Gelatine.	Carmine.
2 tablespoonsful Water.	Cream or Custard.

Beat the buttermilk, juice, rind and sugar till latter is dissolved. Colour a pale pink with carmine. Put the gelatine into a pan with the cold water and stir till it dissolves. Add carefully to the buttermilk mixture and strain into a glass dish through a fairly fine strainer. When it has set, decorate with whipped cream well sweetened, or, if preferred, serve with cup custard. This pudding does not taste of buttermilk, but has a fresh lemon flavour very agreeable in hot weather.

ORANGE SPONGE. (186)

2½ ozs. Marshall's Semolina.	2 tablespoonsful Sugar.
1 pint Water.	Pinch of Salt.
4 blood Oranges.	

Grate the rind of 2 oranges into the water, squeeze the juice of the 4 and set aside.

Put on the water and let it come slowly to the boil. Sprinkle in the semolina, let it boil 8 minutes, and then add the sugar and mix well. Take off the fire and add the orange juice, which should be strained, and then the salt. Pour into a basin and whip steadily with a wire whisk for 20 minutes and pour into a wet mould.

ECONOMICAL LEMON SPONGE. (187)

A still more economical dish can be made by using 2 ozs. Marshall's Semolina to the pint of water, and after boiling 8 minutes remove from the fire and add 1½ teaspoons Essence of Lemon and sugar to taste. Beat 20 minutes and mould. Serve with custard sauce.

JELLY SPONGE. (188)

Some people are unaware that a jelly can be whipped up and will, in a few minutes, produce an excellent sponge. A bottle or packet of table jelly is dissolved in the usual way in a fair sized basin and just as it begins to set should be beaten with a " Dover " beater or a wire whisk till a thick sponge is formed and then set in moulds. As the bulk is considerably increased in whipping a mould larger than the jelly should be used. This pudding can be made in at least eight flavours and is capable of producing a great variety of cold sweets in conjunction with tinned or stewed fruits, custards, etc. Some of the jelly may be allowed to set in a small basin and when quite stiff this makes a pretty garnish if chopped with a sharp knife and laid round the base of the sponge when turned out.

GROUND RICE CARAMEL.   (189)

1 pint Milk.	2 ozs. Ground Rice.
1 oz. Loaf Sugar.	Lemon Rind.

CARAMEL.—$\frac{3}{4}$ ozs. Sugar.
$\frac{3}{4}$ gill Water.

To prepare the caramel put the water and sugar into a small dry pan and let it cook over the fire, without stirring, till it becomes a rich brown colour. Have a plain tin mould heated and at once pour the caramel into it and quickly coat the tin with it, turning it round and round to cover the sides.

Put the milk into a saucepan and add the loaf sugar very well rubbed on the lemon rind, and when the milk boils, sprinkle in the ground rice and let it cook for ten minutes. Pour this into the prepared mould, cover with greased paper and steam for 20 minutes. When *cold*, turn out, and the caramel will fall round and form a sauce.

HONEYCOMB CREAM.   (190)

3 gills Milk.	2 Eggs.
$\frac{1}{2}$ oz. Cox's Powdered Gelatine.	2 tablespoonsful Sugar.
$\frac{1}{2}$ teaspoonful Vanilla Essence.	

Beat the yolks of the eggs and the sugar (which should be castor) till creamy. Whip the whites very stiffly. Dissolve the gelatine in the milk till nearly boiling point, but on no account allow it to boil. Strain on to the yolks, sugar and vanilla, mix well, and lastly, fold in the whites of egg which should be given a final whip up just before adding. Pour into a wetted mould to set.

RUM JUNKET. (191)

This is one of the most delicious junkets, and, in common with most other junkets, is extremely simple to prepare.

1 pint New Milk.	1 gill Cream.
1 tablespoonful Rum.	Ground Cinnamon.
1 teaspoonful Essence of Rennet.	Vanilla and Sugar.

Warm the milk and rum to blood heat and add the rennet. Mix and pour into glass dish. When it is set dust it over rather thickly with powdered cinnamon. Whip up the cream, sweeten and flavour it to taste and arrange on top of the junket.

LEMON SOUFFLÉ. (192)

4 ozs. Sugar.	½ gill Water.
¾ oz. Cox's PowderedGelatine.	Pistachio Nuts.
3 Eggs. ½ pint Cream.	2 Lemons.

Fix a double band of paper firmly round a china soufflé dish so that it comes two inches above the top of the dish. Put the yolks of the eggs and the sugar into a basin and beat them over hot water till thick and creamy. Take from fire and continue beating till almost cold. Add the rind of the lemon very carefully grated to prevent any white getting in. Strain in the juice of the lemons and mix well. Dissolve the gelatine in the water and strain it in, then fold in 1½ gills of the cream lightly whipped and, last of all, the very stiffly beaten whites of eggs. Pour into prepared soufflé dish and lay on ice or in a very cold place till set. Carefully remove the paper band using a sharp knife and wetting it if it shows signs of sticking. Whip the remaining ½ gill of cream and sweeten it, then pipe on to the top of the soufflé. Decorate with slices of blanched pistachio nuts arranged in the form of shamrocks. Lay on lace paper in an entrée dish and serve as cold as possible.

MERINGUE PUDDING. (193)

2 ozs. Flour.	3 ozs. Canton Ginger.
2 ozs. Butter.	3 ozs. Sugar.
2 Eggs.	1 pint Milk.

Cut the ginger into small pieces. Mix the flour perfectly smooth with a little of the milk and put the remainder on to boil. Add butter, ginger, and one ounce of sugar to the milk, and when it boils pour over the flour, keeping it quite free from lumps with beating. Return to saucepan and boil gently for 10 minutes. Let it cool a little and add the yolks of eggs beaten. Grease a pie-dish and pour mixture in. Whip the whites of eggs to a very stiff froth and add the remaining 2 ozs. of sugar to them by degrees— it should be castor. Pile the meringue roughly over the pudding and set in a rather cool oven to harden. Serve cold.

NORWEGIAN CREAM. (194)

If cream substitute is used this pudding requires no sugar, and it can be prepared at short notice. In most store cupboards a few tins of fruit and milk are kept in readiness for emergencies. Variety can be had by using pears and peaches in place of apricots.

1 tin Apricots.	1 gill Milk.
$\frac{1}{2}$ oz. Gelatine.	1$\frac{1}{2}$ gills Cream.
Vanilla Essence.	Sugar.

Chopped Almonds.

Put the apricots and juice into an earthenware or enamelled saucepan and cook gently till quite soft—about 15 minutes. Set aside to cool. Mix the gelatine in the cold milk and stir over a gentle heat till dissolved. Add this gradually to the cool apricots and pour into a glass dish. When it has set, cover with the cream whipped and sweetened and flavoured with vanilla. Decorate with chopped almonds.

PRUNES AND PRISMS. (195)

" Papa, potatoes, poultry, prunes and prisms are all very good words for the lips, especially prunes and prisms."

" LITTLE DORRIT."

This cold sweet undoubtedly owes its name to the above well known quotation of Dickens.

½ lb. Prunes.	1 oz. Flour.
4 ozs. Almonds.	1 Walnut of Butter.
2 ozs. Sugar.	Pinch of Cinnamon.
1 gill Milk.	Juice of 1 Lemon.

1 pint Lemon or Wine Jelly.

Soak prunes overnight in just sufficient water to cover. If not soft enough to stone easily, steam in the same basin for an hour till tender. Cool and remove the stones with lengthwise slits. Boil the other ingredients till quite stiff—about 10 minutes—stirring carefully to avoid burning. Let this mixture cool and stuff the prunes with a small teaspoonful to each. Set each prune in a tiny octagon mould of lemon or wine jelly. When set turn out and garnish with chopped jelly.

APRICOT FOOL. (196)

The following is a very simple but delicious way of serving apricots :—

1 pint Apricot Purée.	1 gill Cream or Milk.
1 oz. Almonds.	

Sieve sufficient apricots and juice to made 1 pint. Add the cream to it. Mix well and serve in custard glasses. Decorate with the almonds blanched and cut in strips.

Serve with savoy biscuits.

RHUBARB FOOL. (197)

When the rhubarb is young and a good colour this makes quite a nice sweet.

To every pound of rhubarb allow ½ pint of custard or ¼ pint custard and ¼ pint cream if expense need not be considered. Wipe the rhubarb and cut in inch lengths, lay it in a jar and add sugar to taste. Cover and cook in the oven till tender, or if more convenient steam it in a jar. Pass through a fine sieve and mix with the custard. Serve in custard glasses with finger biscuits.

BANANA SNOW. (198)

6 Bananas.	1 White of Egg.
Juice of 1 Lemon.	2 tablespoonsful Castor
Shelled Walnuts.	Sugar.

Mash bananas with a silver fork and add lemon juice. Add the sugar and the white of egg stiffly beaten and beat all together till sugar is dissolved. Serve in a glass dish or in custard glasses, and garnish with halves of shelled walnuts.

CHESTNUTS AND ORANGE COMPOTE. (199)

1 lb. Chestnuts.	½ oz. Sugar.
½ gill Milk.	Rind of ½ Lemon.
½ gill Water.	

Split the chestnuts and boil them for 10 minutes. Remove the outer and inner skins. Put them into a stewpan with the lemon rind which should be very thinly cut, and the milk, sugar and water. Cook gently till perfectly tender, remove the lid and let them cook till the milk is absorbed. Pass through a sieve on to the dish they are to be served on and decorate to taste.

COMPOTE.

| 4 Sweet Oranges. | Small teacupful Water. |
| 1/2 glass Madeira. | Small teacupful Sugar. |

Cut the oranges and lay in a glass dish with the juice that has run from them. Boil the sugar and water together for 10 minutes and let it get cold. Add the Madeira and pour over the oranges. Serve very cold. Do not prepare the oranges too long before they are wanted.

COMPOTE OF FIGS.   (200)

1 lb. Figs.	1 dessertspoonful Lemon
6 ozs. Sugar.	Juice.
1/2 pint Water.	1 glass Claret.

Wash the figs very carefully and reject any that are black or discoloured. Cut off the stems at the ends. Put into a strong jar and soak all night in the water.

Next day add to them the sugar, lemon juice and claret and let all steam in a saucepan with water to come half way up the jar. They may take any time from 1 to 2 hours, according to the kind of figs, but they should be perfectly tender before dishing.

Put the figs in a glass dish and boil up the syrup quickly, to reduce it considerably, then pour over the figs.

RHUBARB AND RAISIN COMPOTE.   (201)

2 lbs. Rhubarb.	2 1/2 gills Boiling Water.
4 ozs. Sultanas.	Lemon Juice.
Sugar.	

Pick and wash the sultanas—the large Australian ones are excellent for this dish. Put into an earthenware dish with the boiling water, put on a lid and let them stew gently till only about 1/2 gill water remains.

Wipe the rhubarb and cut it into inch lengths and add it to the raisins with sugar to taste and about 2 teaspoonsful of lemon juice and mix well.   Cook slowly in the oven till the rhubarb is tender but not broken.

Rhubarb and raisin tart is delicious.   The raisins should be prepared as above and then added to the rhubarb in the pie-dish and covered with a good short crust.

GOOSEBERRY FOOL.   (202)

1 lb. Green Gooseberries.	1 gill Cream or Milk.
¼ lb. Sugar.	1 gill Water.
Ratafia Biscuits.	

Wash and pick gooseberries and stew in the water and sugar till quite soft.   Pass through a hair or fine wire sieve.   When cold add the cream or milk to the pulp. Serve as cold as possible in custard glasses and decorate each with ratafia biscuits.

PEAR WHIPS.   (203)

½ lb. Dried Pears.	1 dessertspoonful Lemon Juice.
2 dessertspoonsful Castor Sugar.	1 white of Egg.
	Almond Rock.

Wash the pears very well in warm water and put into a small basin.   Cover them with boiling water and put a plate on the top.   When they are cold put bowl into a pan with boiling water and steam till quite tender. Drain on a sieve and when free from juice pass through the sieve.

Whip the white of egg till very stiff, add the sugar, lemon juice and pear purée and whip till sugar is dissolved. It will take about 5 minutes.   Serve in custard glasses and sprinkle with crushed French almond rock.   Keep in a cool place so that whips are as cold as possible when served.

RASPBERRY CUPS. (204)

6 Bananas.	1 oz. Sugar.
½ lb. Raspberries.	Cream.

Peel and scrape bananas, slice across with a silver knife and lay in six custard glasses.

Sieve the raspberries, mix with the sugar and stir occasionally till it is dissolved. Pour over the bananas and put a spoonful of whipped cream on and serve as cold as possible with finger biscuits.

SUN DRIED FRUITS. (205)

These are valuable when few fresh ones are in season for cooking purposes. Being ripe fruits, dried in the sun, they are much less sour than fresh fruits and consequently require less sugar in cooking.

The best results are got by slow stewing in an earthenware jar in the oven, or failing that, by steaming in a basin in a saucepan with boiling water.

To prepare the fruit, scald it first with boiling water and then wash thoroughly in cold water. Cover with cold water and soak for 24 hours. Cook very slowly for 1 to 2 hours, according to the fruit used. Three tablespoons sugar to the pound of fruit is usually sufficient to make a nice syrup, but it should not be added till fruit is nearly cooked. If a thicker syrup is desired, place the fruit in a glass dish and reduce the syrup by fast boiling and when cold pour over the fruit.

Cloves, cinnamon, nutmeg, lemon rind and juice may all be added for variety. Pears require less soaking but peaches should be soaked 48 hours and peeled before cooking.

SEEDLESS RAISINS.   (206)

Considering their food value, it is surprising to find how few people make use of the excellent Californian seedless raisins which are sent over in small packages weighing about one pound.   They have a rich, fruity flavour and require little or no sugar in cooking.

COMPOTE OF RAISINS.   (207)

¾ lb. Seedless Raisins. | 2 gills Cold Water.

Pick the raisins, wash and put into a pudding basin with half a pint of water.   Cover with a paper, put a saucer on top and place in a saucepan with sufficient water to come half way up the basin, and steam steadily for 2 hours. Turn out, and, when cold, serve with cream, custard, or milk pudding.

RAISIN FOOL.   (208)

½ lb. Seedless Raisins. | ½ pint Cup Custard.
1 gill Water. | Sugar.

Steam the raisins in the water, in the method given for compote of raisins, and pass through a wire sieve.   Make half a pint of custard and sweeten to taste.   When cold, mix well with the sieved raisins and serve in custard glasses.

CHOCOLATE RAISIN FOOL.   (209)

Proceed as for raisin fool, but in making the custard add a dessertspoonful chocolate powder, and before serving dust the tops of the glasses with powdered cinnamon.

AN ECONOMICAL STRAWBERRY CREAM. (210)

1 pint packet Strawberry Jelly.	½ gill Cream.
Boiling Water.	Candied Fruits.
1 gill Libby's Evaporated Milk.	

Since cream is so expensive this makes a useful sweet for children's parties, etc., and it also makes quite a good filling for a charlotte Russe. Divide the jelly in two and dissolve one half in ½ pint boiling water. When it is cold line the bottom of a wetted mould with a thin layer of it ; when this is set arrange a neat decoration of candied fruits on it and set these with a second layer of jelly. Put the remainder of the jelly in a cold place to set. Melt the second half of the jelly in 1 gill of boiling water and when it is cold, but not set, add the cream and the evaporated milk. With a wire whisk beat slowly and steadily for seven minutes and pour into the prepared mould.

When it is set turn out and garnish with the remaining jelly chopped and arranged in little heaps round the cream.

A less rich sweet can be made in the same way using 1½ gills of Libby's milk and no cream.

TUTTI FRUTTI. (211)

This is a pleasant form of fruit salad and very suitable for occasions where a considerable quantity is required. Take a deep bowl which can be sent to table and lay in closely together enough macaroons or ratafias to cover the botton. Then add to it a good layer of peaches or apricots then one of dark cherries then pears then raspberries or loganberries. Cover with a layer of macaroons and pour a pint of cup custard over all. Decorate with a cross of crushed ratafias picked out with candied violets.

CAKES, SCONES, Etc.

APPLE SAUCE CAKE. (212)

8 ozs. Flour.
4 ozs. Castor Sugar.
4 ozs. Butter.
1 teaspoonful Bi-Carb. of Soda.
1 teaspoonful Ground Cinnamon.

4 ozs. Sultanas.
1 dessertspoonful hot Water.
1 small teaspoonful Ground
Cloves.
Saltspoonful of Salt.

1 teacupful sour Apple Sauce.

This is an American recipe and it makes a rich, spicy and rather moist cake which requires no eggs. The quantity of spice given above is somewhat reduced from the original recipe and of course can be still more so if preferred.

Prepare the sour apple sauce by stewing apples without sugar in a closely covered saucepan, using no more water than is absolutely necessary to prevent them burning ; when soft pass through a fine sieve. ·Cream the butter and sugar till very light. Add the sultanas, salt and spices and mix well. Dissolve the soda in the hot water and pour it into the apple sauce. Hold the cup over the basin, stirring quickly, and allow it to foam over the creamed butter and sugar. Add the flour, which should be sieved, and beat all well together. Pour into a lined loaf tin and bake for about ¾ of an hour.

CEDRIC CAKE. (213)

6 ozs. Flour.
4 ozs. Ground Almonds.
4 ozs. Castor Sugar.
Apricot Jam.

4 ozs. Butter or Margarine.
2 Yolks of Eggs.
Grated Rind of ½ Lemon.

GLACÉ ICING. { ¾ lb. Icing Sugar. Boiling Water. Yellow Colouring. }

Citron Peel.
Chopped Almonds.

Sieve the flour into a basin, add the ground almonds, sugar and lemon rind and mix well. Rub the butter into these and then add the yolks of eggs, unbeaten, and work well with a wooden spoon till a nice paste is formed. Turn on to a floured board and knead well till the paste is quite smooth.

Divide into three pieces and roll each one out about ¼ of an inch thick. Cut into oblong pieces and lay on a paper on a baking tray. Bake in a moderate oven till a pale yellow colour. The flavour will be quite spoiled if they are too much baked. They will take about 20 minutes to bake. When cold spread two of the strips with apricot jam and pile on top on one another. Press together and ice on top and sides with glacé icing flavoured slightly with ratafia and coloured a pale yellow.

Decorate with a round of chopped citron peel and outside this arrange a ring of chopped almonds. The almonds should be blanched, dried and browned lightly in the oven before chopping.

CHRISTMAS CAKE. (214)

As this excellent cake should be kept for some time before cutting it is none too soon to prepare it in October for Christmas. The almond paste and icing should not be put on till a few days before it is to be used. The cake itself will keep good for a year.

1 lb. Flour.	1 lb. Currants.
¾ lb. Butter.	½ lb. Mixed Peel.
¾ lb. Demerara Sugar.	1 teaspoonful Borwick's Baking
2 ozs. Sweet Almonds.	Powder.
6 Eggs.	1 gill Milk.
1 tablespoonful Brandy.	1 gill Treacle.
1 lb. Sultanas.	

Line a cake tin with greased paper and dust it out with flour. Clean and pick the fruit and shred the peel. Blanch and shred the almonds. Mix the milk and treacle together and warm them slightly. Sieve the flour. Cream the butter and sugar till very light, add a little flour and an unbeaten egg and beat very well. Add more flour and some of the treacle mixture. Continue till all is used up. Add the fruit and the baking powder with the last of the flour. Beat all very thoroughly and then add the brandy. Bake 2½ to 3 hours in a steady oven. When cold store in a tin with close fitting lid.

DATE AND WALNUT CAKE.   (215)

1 lb. Cooking Dates.	½ lb. Margarine or Butter.
¼ lb. Shelled Walnuts.	1 teacupful Castor Sugar.
2 teacups Flour.	2/3rds teacupful Milk.
½ teaspoonful Bi-Carbonate of	2 Eggs.
Soda.	

Wash, dry and stone the dates and cut up roughly. Break up walnuts (not too fine) with the fingers, and sieve the flour. Cream butter and sugar till very light, add eggs singly with some of the flour, and beat each very well. Mix walnuts and dates and add with last of flour dusted through them. Heat the milk, dissolve the soda in it and add last of all. Bake in a moderate oven in a rather shallow tin as the cake should only be about 2 inches high. If possible do not cut for a day or two after baking.

DUNDEE CAKE. (216)

¾ lb. Flour.	Milk to mix.
½ lb. Margarine.	¼ lb. Lemon Peel.
6 ozs. Sugar.	1 teaspoonful Treacle.
1 lb. Currants,	1 teaspoonful Vinegar.
¼ lb. Sultanas.	½ teaspoonful Bi-Carb. of Soda.
3 flat tablespoonsful Cook's	½ teaspoonful Cream of Tartar.
Eggs or 3 fresh Eggs.	Pinch of Salt.

Clean the currants and sultanas in a little flour and pick carefully. Cut the peel in shreds. Cream the margarine and sugar. Add the eggs and sieved flour alternately. Mix fruit and other dry ingredients with last of flour. Add treacle and sufficient milk to make a nice dough. Add vinegar last of all. Bake in a tin lined with greased paper for 3 hours, in a steady oven, reducing the heat after the first hour. Do not cut the cake for a day or two.

" GOODGE." (217)

Those people who consider it well nigh impossible to make a good cake with neither eggs nor milk will find in this recipe a cake which is quite as much appreciated in the dining room as it is in the nursery or school-room. It keeps soft in a tin, and is an extremely inexpensive addition to the store cupboard :—

1 cupful Syrup or Treacle, or mixed.	1 teaspoonful Bi.-Carb. of Soda.
	12 ozs. Flour.
2 ozs. Margarine.	1 cupful Boiling Water.
2 teaspoonsful Ground Ginger.	

Put a breakfast cupful of syrup and treacle into a good sized basin. Add the margarine broken up small, then the ginger and soda free from lumps. Pour in by degrees a breakfast cupful boiling water and dredge in the flour. When well mixed pour into a greased and floured flat baking tin about 14″ × 10″. Bake in a moderate oven for half an hour. Cool in tin. When cold cut in squares.

" GLORIFIED GOODGE." (218)

1½ cupsful Westburn Syrup.
3 ozs. Margarine.
1¼ cupsful Boiling Water.

1 lb. Flour.
1½ teaspoonsful Bi-Carb. of Soda.
½ lb. Cocoa.

Make like goodge, adding the cocoa before the flour, and bake in a tin 16″ × 12″ from 30 to 40 minutes. When cold cut in squares. Both cakes should cool in the tin.

HAZEL NUT CAKE. (219)

6 ozs. Ground Hazel Nuts.
6 ozs. Castor Sugar.

4 Eggs.
1 oz. Flour.

Beat eggs and sugar for 15 minutes. Sift the flour and add it and the nuts very lightly to the eggs. Pour into a round tin, previously lined with greased and floured paper, and bake in a good oven for 40 minutes.

Dust with icing sugar when cold.

ORANGE SPONGE CAKE. (220)

1 teacupful Flour.
1 teacupful Castor Sugar.
3 Eggs.

1 teaspoonful Baking Powder.
3 tablespoonsful Boiling Water.

Dry, sift and weigh the flour and prepare the tin.

Put sugar into a basin and moisten with the water. Stir for a few seconds then add the eggs and beat steadily with a wire whisk for 20 minutes without stopping.

Add the flour and baking powder lightly and mix well. Do not stir the flour but fold it over and over. Bake in a good oven for almost half an hour. Turn out and while still warm cover with the following icing :—

Icing :—¾ lb. Icing Sugar.
1½ Oranges.
½ Lemon.

Grate the oranges and lemon and mix with the juice and let it stand for an hour, then strain.

Sieve the sugar and gradually beat the juice into it till quite smooth and thick, then spread on cake. Icing to be put on a warm cake should be stiffer than for a cold one as the heat of the cake causes the sugar to run more freely.

PLUM CAKE. (221)

¾ lb. Flour.	¼ teaspoonful Mixed Spice.
½ lb. Butter.	1 teaspoonful Glycerine.
½ lb. Sugar.	1 wineglassful Brandy.
½ lb. Sultanas.	½ teaspoonful Salt.
½ lb. Cherries.	1 teaspoonful Baking Powder.
¼ lb. Sweet Almonds.	6 Eggs.
¼ lb. Mixed Peel.	Grated Rind of 2 Lemons.

Chop almonds roughly. Pick over the sultanas and cherries. Shred the peel and grate the rind of lemons. Sift the flour, cream the butter and sugar very thoroughly. Add the eggs singly with two tablespoons of flour and beat each one well, before adding another. Add fruit, salt, spice and baking powder with last of flour and beat all well together. Add glycerine and brandy last of all. Bake from 3 to 4 hours in a steady oven, reducing the heat after the first hour.

SNOW CAKE. (222)

4 ozs. Castor Sugar.	2 Eggs.
4 ozs. Butter.	Rind of ½ Lemon or Lemon
½ teaspoonful Baking Powder.	Essence.
8 ozs. Potato Flour.	

Cream the butter and sugar till very light and add the lemon rind. Add the eggs singly with a little of the flour and beat each for 5 minutes after adding. Mix the baking powder with the last of the flour. Bake in a steady oven for about an hour.

AYRSHIRE SHORTBREAD.   (223)

3½ ozs. Flour.	1 yolk of Egg.
½ oz. Potato Flour.	2 ozs. Butter.
1 oz. Castor Sugar.	

Scrub the hands very clean and flour them.

Sieve the two flours together and leave ready to hand. Mix the yolk of egg and sugar on a flat dish and add the butter to it. Work these together with the hand and when well mixed add the flour by degrees. Knead this mixture for at least 15 minutes then roll out and cut in rounds or fingers. Bake in a moderate oven for 15 minutes keeping them pale in colour.

SCOTCH SHORTBREAD.   (224)

4 ozs. Flour.	2 ozs. Rice Flour.
4 ozs. Butter.	2 ozs. Castor Sugar.

Sieve the flours into a dry basin, add the sugar and mix together. Put in the butter in a piece and with the hand work the flour into it, kneading it very well. No moisture of any kind should be added, although to a novice it may appear well nigh impossible to make a paste of the ingredients given. When the mixture has become perfectly smooth and leaves the sides of the basin quite clean continue to knead for some minutes, then turn on to a floured board and form into one round cake about half an inch thick. Flute the edges and prick all over with a fork. Lay on a lightly greased and floured tin and bake in a rather slack oven for ¾ of an hour when the shortbread should be a pale yellow colour. Do not remove it from the tin till it is cold.

This shortbread keeps admirably but before using it should be heated through in the oven and allowed to cool, if it is not freshly made.

PITCAITHLEY BANNOCKS.   (225)

These are made by adding an ounce of blanched almonds cut in strips lengthwise and an ounce of finely shredded citron peel to the shortbread mixture given above.

QUAKER OATS SHORTBREAD.   (226)

4 ozs. Quaker or Rolled Oats.	2 ozs. Castor Sugar.
3 ozs. Butter or Margarine.	2 ozs. Flour.

Sieve the flour and sugar into a basin.   Add the oats and mix together.   Add the butter in one piece and with the hand knead the ingredients together till they are quite blended and the mixture leaves the basin clean and is free from cracks.

Form into a cake quite half an inch thick, flute the edges round with the handle of a knife and prick over with a fork to prevent it rising.   If preferred the mixture may be formed into fingers or small rounds of the same thickness and pricked in the same way.

Lay on a sheet of floured paper on a baking tin and bake the larger cakes about half an hour in a moderate oven and the smaller ones in proportion.   This shortbread requires careful baking as it scorches easily and if more than a pale golden colour the flavour will be quite spoiled.

PETITES GATEAUX À LA ALEXANDRA. (227)

Put into a whipping pan

4 large Eggs.	12 drops Vanilla Essence.
4 ozs. Castor Sugar.	1 oz. Powdered Chocolate.

Whip together over a stew pan of boiling water till the mixture is just warm.   Remove from fire and whip till cold and thick then add 3 ozs. finely sifted and warmed flour.

Brush over a sauté pan and line it with buttered paper,

sprinkle with equal quantities flour and sugar and pour in the cake mixture ½ an inch in thickness.

Place the sauté pan in a moderate oven and bake 25-30 minutes. When cold pour a maraschino and coffee glaze over it. Cut into strips about 1½ inches long with a knife dipped in hot water. Decorate with violet butter icing.

MARASCHINO GLAZE. (228)

¾ lb. Icing Sugar.	1½ tablespoonsful Mrs. Marshall's
2 tablespoonsful Warm Water.	Maraschino Syrup.

Just warm over the fire and add a teaspoonful coffee essence. Draw a fork through the glaze, which will give it a mottled appearance.

VIOLET ICING. (229)

2 ozs. Butter.	Violet Vegetable Colouring.
4 ozs. Icing Sugar.	

Pass the sugar through a sieve ; cream the butter and add the sugar by degrees. Colour to taste and pipe on cakes.

COFFEE CAKES. (230)

3 ozs. Flour.	3 ozs. Castor Sugar.
2 ozs. Cornflour.	½ teaspoonful Baking Powder
2 Eggs.	1 tablespoonful Coffee
3 ozs. Butter.	Essence.

Grease 18 small tins and dust them out with flour. Sieve the flour. Cream the butter and sugar and add one whole egg and a spoonful of flour. Beat for 5 minutes, then add the second egg and beat another 5 minutes, then add the coffee essence. Mix the flour, cornflour and baking powder together and add to the mixture, beat quite smooth and rather more than half fill the tins. Bake in a good oven for 20 minutes keeping the cakes light in colour. Arrange on a wire tray and ice.

ICING. (231)

¾ lb. Icing Sugar.	Boiling Water.
1 tablespoonful Coffee Essence.	

Sieve the sugar, add the coffee essence and just sufficient water to make the icing thin enough to coat the back of the spoon. Beat well to make it glossy and pour over the cakes. Decorate to taste.

AFTERNOON TEA SCONES. (232)

To make these scones successfully it is necessary to have everything ready for use and the oven very hot indeed before beginning to mix them.

4 teacups Flour.	3 teaspoonsful Baking Powder.
3 dessertspoonsful Castor Sugar.	About a teacupful of Milk.
1 heaped tablepoonful Butter or Margarine.	1 Egg.
	Pinch of Salt.

Put the baking sheet for the scones into the oven to get hot. Beat the egg till very light and add some of the milk to it. Sieve the flour and baking powder and rub the butter lightly into it till it looks like breadcrumbs. Add sugar and mix it to a soft dough with the egg and milk. Let the dough be as soft as it can be handled. Roll out lightly, but do not work the dough at all. Cut with a small round cutter and place at once on the hot baking sheet and bake for 5 minutes in a very hot oven. Split open, butter and serve at once.

AMERICAN SCONES. (233)

2 teacups Flour.	3 ozs. Butter.
1 teaspoonful Castor Sugar.	1 Egg.
½ teacupful Milk.	1½ teaspoonsful Baking Powder.

Mix dry ingredients. Melt the butter, add well beaten egg and milk. Mix all together. Beat well and bake in patty tins in fast oven for 10-15 minutes. This recipe is excellent for pastry, using less milk.

OVEN SCONES.   (234)

Cream of tartar is one of the things which became much more expensive during the war, and where much baking is done at home a considerable saving can be effected by the use of " Snocreme," which is a most excellent substitute, and makes delicious scones and buns.

½ lb. Flour.	1 dessertspoonful Butter.
1 level teaspoonful Snocreme.	¼ teaspoonful Salt.
½ level teaspoonful Bi-Carb. of Soda.	1 teaspoonful Castor Sugar.
	1 gill Sour Milk.

Sieve dry ingredients. Rub butter into the flour and make into a soft dough with the milk. Cut and lay on a hot baking sheet and bake in the oven till brown. The oven should be rather hot. Sweet milk can be used if more convenient, but milk that has gone sour makes lighter scones.

CHOCOLATE DOUGHNUTS.   (235)

2 Eggs.	½ teaspoonful Salt.
4 ozs. Castor Sugar.	½ teaspoonful Cinnamon.
2 ozs. Margarine,	1½ teaspoonsful Royal Baking Powder
6 tablespoonsful Milk.	Castor Sugar.
½ lb. Flour.	
Chocolate.	

Beat the eggs and sugar with a whisk till very light. Sieve the flour, spice and salt together. Melt the margarine and add to the beaten eggs, then some flour and then the milk. Add the baking powder with the last of the flour and mix well.

Have a pan of deep fat with faint blue smoke rising from it. Drop the mixture into it in teaspoonfuls and fry till a nice brown all over. Drain and toss in a paper with castor sugar and grated chocolate mixed.

COCOANUT BUNS. (236)

These buns are very inexpensive, and much less stodgy than rock buns, and they will be found useful for children's picnic baskets in the holidays.

¾ lb. Flour.	¼ lb. Desiccated Cocoanut.
Small ½ oz. Cream of Tartar.	¼ lb. Castor Sugar.
Small ¼ oz. Bi-Carbonate of Soda	3 ozs. Margarine.
1 gill Milk.	1 Egg.

Sieve the flour and powders through a wire sieve. Beat the egg and add the milk to it. Cream butter and sugar till very light and add liquid and flour by degrees to make rather a stiff mixture. Place in rough heaps on a greased tray and bake in a hot oven for 20 minutes.

N.B.—If " Snocreme " is used 2 level teaspoonsful should be substituted for the cream of tartar and 1 level teaspoonful for ¼ oz. soda.

COFFEE BUNS. (237)

This is an excellent recipe for those useful buns, which keep well if kept in a dry airtight tin.

1 lb. Flour.	1 teaspoonful Baking Powder.
⅓ lb. Margarine or Butter.	¼ lb. Sugar.
2 Eggs.	Handful of Currants.

Sift the flour and baking powder into a shallow basin, add the sugar and currants and mix well. Add the butter and with the hand knead these ingredients well together, adding a little beaten egg from time to time. Continue working like this till a fine smooth paste is formed. Lightly flour a baking board and break off pieces of the paste. With both hands roll out these pieces to about the diameter of a five shilling piece. Cut off slices from the rolls about an inch thick and lay on a greased and floured baking sheet, allowing plenty of room to spread. Glaze with beaten egg, and bake in a good oven 10-12 minutes.

CREAM BISCUITS. (238)

These biscuits are delicious served in place of bread at dinner. The success of them depends upon the very thorough beating of the paste, which should be done at the time least likely to disturb the household.

¼ lb. Flour.	2 tablespoonsful Cream.
½ oz. Butter.	Salt.

Rub the butter into the flour, add the salt and then the cream. Mix well and turn on to a floured marble or wooden board, and beat from 10 to 15 minutes with the rolling pin when a fine smooth paste will be the result. Roll out as thin as possible, and cut into strips about 5 inches by 2, and bake in a quick oven. Serve in toast racks.

GINGER FINGERS. (239)

4 ozs. Margarine.	5 ozs. Flour.
4 ozs. Castor Sugar.	1 oz. Potato Flour.
1 teaspoonful Ground Ginger.	

Sieve the flours and ginger on to a paper. Scrub the hands clean and with the fingers cream the margarine and sugar. When light add the flour mixture and work well in with the fingers. Knead well with the hand till a soft paste is formed. Roll out in a long strip and cut in fingers. Bake in a good oven for 15 or 20 minutes.

QUAKER OAT BISCUITS. (240)

1 cupful Quaker Oats.	½ cupful Melted Butter.
1 cupful Granulated Sugar.	1 Egg, well beaten.

Mix all together and drop on a greased and slightly heated baking sheet, using a teaspoon and placing them far apart. Cook in a moderate oven. The biscuits should be very thin, and they should be allowed to cool on the tin before removing, as they are very brittle.

RICH OATCAKES. (241)

4 handfuls Oatmeal.	1 teaspoonful Salt.
2 handfuls Flaked Maize.	1 teaspoonful Sugar.
¼ lb. Margarine.	Pinch of Bi-Carbonate of Soda.

Mix the dry ingredients thoroughly. Add margarine and with a knife cut up into small pieces. Work into the meal with the finger tips, and when the mixture assumes a crumbly appearance lay half of it on one side and mix the remainder with ½ a gill of *boiling* water. Work in well till the mixture leaves the sides of the bowl. Sprinkle board with oatmeal and roll out mixture fairly thin. Stamp out with scone cutter and bake on a hot girdle. Finish off the second half of the cakes in the same manner.

EGGLESS TEACAKE. (242)

This teacake is inexpensive, very easy to prepare and always much appreciated.

3 ozs. B.C.L. Lard.	4 ozs. Peterkin Self-raising Flour.
3 ozs. Castor Sugar.	4 ozs. Flour.
1 oz. Orange Peel.	2 ozs. Sultanas.
2 ozs. Currants.	Milk.
1 heaped teaspoonful Bird's Egg Substitute.	

Shred the peel, clean and pick the fruit. Cream the lard and sugar till very light. Add a spoonful or two of plain flour and a little of the milk and mix well in this way till used up. Add the fruit and then last of all the self-raising flour and egg substitute sieved together. Use enough milk to form into a dough rather softer than for scones. Bake in a round sandwich tin in a good oven and do not cut for some hours after it is cold.

I

YORKSHIRE CHEESE CAKES. (243)

1 pint New Milk.	1 tablespoonful Candied Peel.
1 teaspoonful Essence of Rennet.	1 oz. Currants.
	1 tablespoonful Butter.
1 Egg.	Sugar to taste.

PASTRY.

½ lb. Flour.	1 teaspoonful Sugar.
5 ozs. Margarine.	½ teaspoonful Salt.
¼ teaspoonful Baking Powder.	

Make some pastry with the quantities given above, and line some patty tins with it. Prick the bottom of each case well to prevent rising, and put a scrap of paper in each with a spoonful of rice. When baked, remove the rice and dry the cases in the oven.

Warm the milk to blood heat and add the rennet. Stir well and drain the whey through a muslin and lay aside. Put the curd into a basin and add the peel, finely minced, and the currants picked and washed. Beat up the egg and add it, and, if necessary, a little milk to form a thick batter. Sweeten to taste. Fill the pastry cases with this and bake a golden brown in a steady oven.

This is the real Yorkshire mixture, but many housewives buy the curd ready made from the farmers' wives in the market.

WALNUT LOAF. (244)

4 teacupsful Flour.	4 teaspoonsful Baking Powder.
¼ lb. Shelled Walnuts.	¾ teacupful Brown Sugar.
Pinch of Salt.	1½ teacupsful Milk.

Chop the walnuts roughly. Sieve the flour and baking powder and mix all dry things together. Add the milk, mix well, and pour into a greased and floured oblong tin. Bake in a steady oven till firm. Test with heated hat pin.

4 ozs. of seedless raisins make a pleasant variety and richer loaf.

Do not cut the loaf for 24 hours.

SHELFORD LOAF.   (245)

¾ lb. Flour.	1½ ozs. Orange Peel.
3 ozs. Sultanas.	3 ozs. Brown Sugar.
1 dessertspoonful Syrup.	Good teacupful of Milk.
Pinch of Salt.	3 teaspoonsful Baking Powder.
3 ozs. Shelled Walnuts.	

Put the syrup to warm.   Sieve the flour, baking powder and salt into a basin and add the sugar.   Flour and pick the sultanas and chop the walnuts small.   Shred the orange peel and mix all with flour.   Add the heated syrup and milk enough to make a nice dough.   Grease very well two cerebos salt tins or straight-necked jam pots (2 lb. size) and dust out with flour.   Two-thirds fill these with the mixture and pack well down.   Bake in a steady oven for about half an hour then test with a heated hat pin.

If the bottom of the loaf shews any sign of sticking to the tin or jar, lay it on a wet cloth for a few minutes and then turn out.

JAMS, MARMALADES, PICKLES, Etc.

APRICOT JAM. (246)

This recipe is useful for small households where only a few pots of each sort of jam are wanted.

1 lb. Dried Apricots.	4 lbs. Sugar.
3 pints Water.	Rind and juice of 1 or 2 Lemons.

Scald the fruit in boiling water then add a little cold and wash very well. Drain off, cut apricots in two and soak in the measured water for 48 hours.

Peel the rind very thinly, removing all white which makes the jam bitter, and keep the pieces as large as possible.

Put apricots, water and rind into a preserving pan and bring to the boil. Simmer for half an hour then remove the lemon rind and add the sugar and strained lemon juice. After boiling these for 20 minutes test in the usual way. The jam will take from 20 to 30 minutes to do—much depends upon the sugar.

Pot and cover at once.

BLACK CURRANT JAM. (247)

To preserve the flavour of the fruit in jam making it is a great mistake to boil the sugar for any length of time with the fruit. The skins of black currants are rather tough and require some cooking, but the sugar should not be added until after this is done.

This recipe makes excellent jam which keeps well. The proportions are :—

1 pint Currants.	1¼ lbs. Sugar.
¼ pint Water.	

Boil the currants and water gently for 20 minutes till quite cooked. Then add the sugar, let it come slowly to the boil and boil *fast* for three minutes. Pot and cover at once.

BRAMBLE JELLY. (248)

Pick over and wash the brambles, which should not be too ripe. Put them in a preserving pan and pour cold water on them till it begins to appear through the berries. Bring slowly to the boil and simmer gently for half an hour. Strain through a jelly bag and measure the juice. To each pint of juice allow 1 lb. cane sugar and boil for 15 minutes.

GOOSEBERRY JAM. (249)

This jam is often very thick and full of skins, but made from this recipe it will be found to have more jelly and still be perfectly firm.

2 pints Water.	6 lbs. Sugar.
4 lbs. Gooseberries.	

Wash and pick the gooseberries and put into preserving pan with the water and sugar. Stir carefully to prevent burning and boil steadily for 30 minutes. Pot and cover at once.

RASPBERRY JAM   (250)

To each pound of ripe raspberries allow a pound of pure cane sugar. Put into preserving pan together and mash fruit well with spoon while stirring. Boil fast for 3 minutes. Pot and cover at once. Jam made in this way has a much better colour and a delicious fresh flavour, and loses much less in cooking.

STRAWBERRY JAM.   (251)

Many people complain that their strawberry jam does not thicken well, but if the following method is employed they will find it as stiff as anyone could wish. To every pound of dry hulled strawberries allow 1 lb. sugar. Boil very fast for 10 minutes, pot and cover at once.

TOMATO JAM.   (252)

This jam is particularly good for open tarts, but unless one grows tomatoes it cannot be considered at all an economical jam.

2 lbs. Tomatoes.	1 lb. Valencia Raisins.
1 lb. Apples.	¼ lb. Candied Peel.
4 lbs. Sugar.	Juice of 1 Lemon.

Skin red tomatoes by pouring boiling water on them. Peel and chop the apples very small and stew gently with the tomato pulp till soft. Stone and half the raisins, shred the peel finely and add with the sugar to the pulp. Boil gently for half an hour, then add the lemon juice. Mix well, pot, and cover at once. Apples and tomatoes should be weighed after preparing.

VEGETABLE MARROW JAM.   (253)

6 lbs. Marrow.	6 lbs. Sugar.
3 Lemons.	1½ oz. Whole Ginger.

Choose firm and not over ripe marrows. Peel, free from seeds, etc., and cut in pieces about an inch thick and a couple of inches long. Put into a deep basin and sprinkle sugar between each layer. Let it stand 24 hours. Bruise and cut up the ginger and put on with the marrow and sugar. Let it boil gently till the marrow is clear. The time depends upon the marrow, but it will take at least 50 minutes to 1 hour. Add the juice and grated rind of the lemons just before dishing and divide the ginger equally amongst the pots. Many people add a glass of whisky with the lemons. Cover the jam hot.

SEVILLE ORANGE MARMALADE. (254)

3½ lbs. Oranges.	Sugar.
3 Lemons.	Water.

Scrub the oranges and lemons perfectly clean with a brush, dry them and, with a sharp knife, cut them down in very thin slices. Keep one basin for the pulp and one for the pips and above all keep the knife well sharpened as it saves much time and trouble.

Weigh the pulp and to each pound allow 3 pints of cold water, put all into a deep pan or basin and let it stand for 24 hours. Out of this quantity of water take sufficient to well cover the pips and let them stand for 24 hours also.

Next day boil the pulp gently till tender. It will take about 1½ hours and it should not boil fast or it will reduce too much. Simmer the pips in a covered pan for an hour and strain juice into the pulp. Let it stand for another 24 hours then weigh and allow 1 lb. of sugar to each pound of pulp. Boil steadily for an hour and stir fairly constantly to prevent scum settling on the top. Test in the usual way, pot and cover at once.

OXFORD MARMALADE. (255)

For those who like the thick bitter marmalade usually
known by this name the same method applies but the
fruit should be cut a trifle thicker and only two pints of
water allowed to each pound of fruit.

GOLDEN MARMALADE. (256)

2 Grape Fruit.	2 Seville Oranges.
2 Lemons.	Sugar.
Water.	

Scrub the fruit and dry it. Cut the grape fruit in
quarters and remove the core. Slice it and the oranges
and lemons very thinly indeed. Put the pips into a small
basin. Weigh the pulp and allow three pints of cold
water to each pound of fruit. Out of this water take
sufficient to well cover the pips. Let all stand for 24
hours. Boil the fruit, not too fast, for 1½ hours or till
perfectly tender. Simmer the pips in a covered pan for
an hour and strain the liquid into the fruit pulp. Let all
stand another 24 hours then weigh and allow a pound of
sugar to each pound of pulp. Boil rather quickly for an
hour then test and, if ready, pot and cover at once.

ORANGE JELLY. (257)

6 lbs. of Oranges.	14 pints of Water.
1 lb. of Lemons.	

Scrub the fruit perfectly clean with a brush and dry it.
Cut the oranges and lemons into slices, lay in a deep basin,
pour on the cold water, and soak for 24 hours. Next day
boil for 1½ hours. Strain through a flannel jelly bag.
Weigh the juice and to every pound of juice allow 1 lb. of
loaf sugar. Watch carefully when it comes to the boil,
skim, and boil for 9 minutes.

TANGERINE AND LEMON JELLY. (258)

4 lbs. Tangerines.	Water.
2 lbs. Lemons.	Sugar.

For this jelly choose tangerines which are not very ripe. Wipe the oranges and lemons clean with a damp cloth and with a sharp knife cut into slices. Weigh the fruit, pips and all, and to each pound of pulp allow 2 pints of water. Let the fruit stand in the water for 24 hours then boil steadily for an hour. Do not boil fast as it reduces the water too much. Strain the pulp through a jelly bag and weigh the juice. To each pound of juice allow 1 lb. of sugar. Put all into a jelly pan and boil fairly fast for 7 minutes. Put into small pots and cover at once.

This jelly should be made before the oranges get too old. It will be found to be considerably sweeter than Seville orange jelly but very refreshing.

APPLE CHUTNEY. (259)

4 lbs. Sour Apples.	1 oz. Garlic.
2 lbs. Moist Sugar.	1½ ozs. Ground Ginger.
1 lb. Raisins.	1 lb. Dates.
¼ oz. Cayenne Pepper.	2 ozs. Salt.
2 quart bottles Brown Vinegar.	

Weigh the apples after peeling and coring. Slice them and cook gently in the vinegar till soft. Stone the raisins and dates, weigh them and cut up roughly. Peel the garlic then weigh it and pound with the salt. When the apples are soft add these ingredients with the sugar, ginger and pepper and cook for 25 minutes, stirring frequently to prevent burning. Put into perfectly dry bottles, and when cold cork and seal. The flavour of this chutney is much improved by keeping and it should stand for at least a couple of months before being used.

SPICED BEETROOT.   (260)

8 small Beetroot.	1 dessertspoonful Whole
1 lb. Brown Sugar.	Cloves.
1 pint Vinegar.	$\frac{1}{2}$ oz. Cinnamon Stick.

Choose small beetroot of equal size. Wash well and cook in boiling water till tender being careful not to let them bleed. Drain them, skin in the usual way and remove the end.

Boil the vinegar with the sugar and spices for 20 minutes then add the beetroot cut in four lengthwise and heat all to boiling point. Put into wide necked bottles and cork firmly.

This makes an excellent sweet pickle much appreciated by those who object to the harshness of the usual pickled beetroot.

SPICED PLUMS.   (261)

4 lbs. Plums.	1 teaspoonful Ground Cloves.
2 lbs. Brown Sugar.	1 teaspoonful Ground Allspice.
1 pint Vinegar.	1 teaspoonful Ground Cinnamon.

Wipe and stone the plums. Make a syrup of the vinegar, sugar and spices, and when it has boiled or 5 minutes add the plums. Let it simmer very gently for 15 to 30 minutes, according to the variety of plums used. They must be tender, but not smashed. Put into small bottles. Cork and seal at once.

GREEN TOMATO PICKLE.   (262)

This is an excellent recipe, and most useful for using up home grown tomatoes which have not ripened. Even when the tomatoes have to be purchased, this makes quite an inexpensive pickle :—

10 lb. Green Tomatoes.	$\frac{1}{4}$ oz. White Pepper Corns.
1 quart bottle White Vinegar.	Salt.
1 quart bottle Brown Vinegar.	2 lbs. Brown Sugar.
$\frac{1}{2}$ teaspoonful Cayenne Pepper.	1 lb. Onions.
$\frac{1}{4}$ oz. Whole Cloves.	$\frac{1}{4}$ oz. Ground Cinnamon.

Wipe the tomatoes and remove any stems. Slice them about three-eights of an inch thick and lay in a basin sprinkling each layer with salt. Let them stand all night then drain off the liquor. Peel and slice the onions very thinly, and mix the cayenne and ground cinnamon perfectly smooth with some of the vinegar. Put all the ingredients into a preserving pan and stir carefully to prevent burning. Allow to simmer gently till quite tender. Let it cool and then bottle. Cork firmly and seal the bottles. This pickle improves with keeping if it is properly corked and sealed.

PRESERVED TOMATOES. (263)

This is a very good recipe, and is useful to the ever-increasing number of persons who grow their own tomatoes, and have quantities ripening at once.

These tomatoes are excellent eaten with mutton in place of red currant jelly.

The proportions are :—

1 lb. Tomatoes.	¼ pint Water.
½ lb. Sugar.	1 Lemon.

Boil the sugar and water for 5 minutes and skim, if necessary. Wipe the tomatoes, which should be sound and firm, and as much of one size as possible. Put into the syrup and cook till tender. Lay on a flat dish to cool. Add the lemon, sliced, and free from pips, to the syrup and boil up once. Put the tomatoes in fruit bottles and pour the hot syrup and lemon over them and screw up tight. They keep well and are generally better the second year than when first made.

TOMATO SAUCE. (264)

3½ lbs. Tomatoes.	1 oz. Garlic.
½ lb. Sugar.	½ oz. Black Peppercorns.
¼ lb. Salt.	¼ oz. Cayenne Pepper.
1 pint Vinegar.	½ oz. Whole Cloves.

Slice the tomatoes and the garlic and let them stew gently with the salt, sugar and spices for half an hour, when the mixture will begin to thicken. Pass through a fine sieve. Add the vinegar and boil slowly for 10 minutes. Bottle when cool, cork firmly, trim off level with top of bottle, and dip in heated wax.

VEGETABLE MARROW PICKLE. (265)

This makes an exceedingly inexpensive pickle, and will perhaps commend itself to housewives who wish to use up marrows otherwise than by making jam.

4 lbs. Marrow.	6 Chillies.
¾ oz. Ground Ginger.	2 doz. Shallots (about ¾ lb.).
1½ oz. Ground Mustard.	½ doz. Cloves.
½ oz. Turmeric.	3 pints Vinegar.
½ lb. Cane Sugar.	Salt.

Weigh the marrow after removing skin and seeds. Cut it up in cubes of about ¾ of an inch and put in a deep basin, sprinkling with salt between each layer. Let it stand over night then strain it off. Chop up the shallots quite small and mix all the remaining ingredients with the vinegar and let it boil in a preserving pan for 10 minutes. Add the marrow to this and simmer till tender. It will take roughly about half an hour, but all depends on the age of the marrow used.

When it is cold put into pickle bottles. Cork firmly and dip in melted wax. This quantity usually fills seven of the smaller size square bottles used by pickle manufacturers.

MISCELLANEOUS RECIPES AND HOUSEHOLD HINTS.

ICINGS FOR CHRISTMAS CAKE.

ALMOND ICING. (266)

1½ lbs. Ground Almonds.	1 Raw Egg.
1 lb. Castor Sugar.	Lemon Juice.

A few drops Orange Flower or Cold Water.

Put almonds and sugar into a mortar or strong basin and pound to a nice consistency with the egg and water, which should be added sparingly. Flavour to taste with lemon juice and spread on cake, making it all perfectly smooth with a knife.

ICING. (267)

2 lbs. Icing Sugar.	Juice of 2 Lemons.
4 Whites of Eggs.	

Pass the sugar through a hair sieve, add the whites of eggs and lemon juice. Work these together with a wooden spoon till perfectly smooth and beat for about 15 minutes till light and creamy then ice the cake with it. Dip a palette knife in hot water from time to time and with this spread the icing on the sides of the cake.

Decorate with crystallised fruits and pistachio nuts blanched and cut in slices and formed into shamrock leaves.

PARISIAN SWEETS. (268)

1 lb. Figs.	1 lb. Shelled Walnuts.
1 lb. Dates.	Icing Sugar.

Remove the stems from figs. Wash, dry and stone the dates, using the soft cooking ones rather than table dates. Mix these together with the walnuts and put through a very fine mincer. Mix well again. Have a baking board dredged with sieved icing sugar.   On this lay the fruit and knead into a cake.   Roll out about ½ an inch thick and cut into squares like caramels.   Toss in icing sugar till well coated and store in tins with parchment paper between the layers.

These sweets look very nice cut like dominoes and coated with white water icing and the pips marked off with chocolate icing.

WALNUT TABLET.   (269)

2 lbs. Granulated Sugar.	4 ozs. Shelled Walnuts.
2 tablespoonsful Golden Syrup.	2 teaspoonsful Vanilla Essence.
2 teacups Sweet Milk.	

Put the milk, sugar and syrup into a fairly large pan and stir it over a good heat till it boils.   Let it boil *fast* for 15 minutes then test in cold water and if it can be formed into a soft ball it can be taken from the fire, if not continue to boil and test till this stage is reached, stirring occasionally.   Much depends on the sugar and the speed with which it is boiled.   When it is taken from the fire add the walnuts chopped and the vanilla essence and beat it without stopping till it begins to feel slightly sugary on the bottom of the pan then pour into a well greased tin. When half cold cut as desired.   This will make about 3 lbs. tablet.

MINCE MEAT.   (270)

1 lb. Raisins.	¼ lb. Sultanas.
1 lb. Currants.	2½ lbs. Apples.
1 lb. Moist Sugar.	1 lb. Suet.
¼ oz. Mixed Spice.	1 Nutmeg (grated).
Juice of 2 Lemons.	2 ozs. Orange Peel.
Rind of 1 Lemon.	2 ozs. Lemon Peel.
¼ lb. Almonds.	2 ozs. Citron Peel.
1 gill Brandy.	1 gill Sherry.
1 gill Port.	

Blanch and chop the almonds, shred the suet very finely and then chop it, removing all skin. Stone and chop the raisins roughly. Peel and chop the apples finely. Shred and peel very finely then mix all very well together, adding the brandy and wine last of all. Put into dry jars, cover with parchment paper and tie securely.

DESSERT PRUNES. (271)

½ pint Gin.	3 tablespoonsful Brown Candy Sugar.
½ pint Boiling Water.	2 lbs. Bottle Prunes.

Separate the fruit and pack lightly into the bottle. As the bottles are very tightly packed it will be necessary to use a second and smaller bottle for the remaining prunes. Dissolve the sugar in the boiling water and then add the gin. Put a lid on and bring quickly to boiling point and at once pour over the prunes and screw down. Let the prunes remain in this for at least a month before using, and, if the top layer of prunes has absorbed the liquid, make sure that the top does not leak, then turn the bottle upside down. Serve in small crystal or china bon-bon dishes.

Only the finest French plums should be used.

FROSTED CURRANTS. (272)

¼ lb. Red Currants.	1 tablespoonful Water.
1 White of Egg.	Castor Sugar.

For this dessert dish use only the choicest currants and arrange the clusters ready to hand. Heat the sugar very slightly. Beat the white of egg and water together and dip the currants into it, drip for a second and coat with the sugar. This is most easily done by heaping the sugar in a soft paper and completely immersing the berries in it, but keeping the ends of the stalks free from the sugar. Shake and lay on a wax paper to dry. Arrange on a dessert dish with fresh leaves.

COCOANUT MILK. (273)

This is very easily prepared from desiccated cocoanut in the following way :—

Put a scant tablespoonful of cocoanut into a small basin and pour over it 1 gill boiling water. Cover and let it stand till cold then strain off for use.

CREAM SUBSTITUTE. (274)

In the country it is sometimes quite impossible to get cream, and as so many cold puddings require it, this substitute may help someone out of her difficulty. Except for the sweetness it is almost impossible to distinguish it from real whipped cream.

½ tin Sweetened Condensed Milk. | Vanilla Essence.
3 ozs. fresh Margarine or Butter. |

Put the margarine and milk in a basin and beat it with a whisk till it is sufficiently stiff to pile up on a dish and keep in shape. Flavour with vanilla essence. This will be found less expensive than fresh cream.

CHESTNUT STUFFING. (275)

¼ lb. Chestnuts. | ¼ lb. Bread Crumbs.
¼ lb. Sausage Meat. | 2 ozs. Suet.
¼ teaspoonful Salt. | ½ teaspoonful Mixed Herbs.
¼ teaspoonful Pepper. | 1 tablespoonful Chopped Parsley
2 tablespoonsful Stock. |

Boil the chestnuts for half an hour and peel them. Pass through a sieve and mix very well with the other ingredients and bind with a little stock. Stuff the turkey with this and sew up.

TOMATO GLAZE. (276)

1 gill Tomato Purée. | Salt and Pepper.
¼ oz. Powdered Gelatine. | Carmine.

Pass some tomatoes through a hair sieve. Dissolve the gelatine in the purée over a gentle heat. Add seasonings and if necessary some carmine. Use when cold.

SPICED PEPPER. (277)

This pepper is excellent for all brown stews and made dishes and for thick brown soups.   There are many people who much prefer it to the ordinary, rather tasteless, white pepper for table use.   The proportions are :—

1 oz. Black Pepper.	2 ozs. Jamaica Pepper.
1 oz. White Pepper.	

If you are fortunate enough to possess a pepper mill buy the black and white pepper corns and pimento berries and grind them at home ; if not, you must use the ordinary ground pepper but it is not nearly so good.   Mix it thoroughly and store in a glass bottle with a stopper or screw top.   It is best to make small quantities at a time.

TO USE UP FAT BACON. (278)

If the bacon for frying is very fat and much is lost in cooking, a saving can be effected by dipping the rashers in flour before frying.

When a piece of very fat bacon is decidedly overboiled and cut very thinly indeed, it is delicious spread on crisp toast and eaten with poached or boiled eggs.   The fat should be so soft that it will spread without any difficulty.

CHEESE FINGERS. (279)

These are quickly and easily prepared and are useful for utilising scraps of pastry left over from pies.

Roll out very thinly any scraps of pastry.   Over half of it sprinkle a good layer of grated cheese and add a dash of cayenne.   Cover with the other half of pastry, prick with a fork, sprinkle with fine salt and cut in fingers.   Bake a pale brown and serve with vegetable purées or salads.

K

VIENNA FINGERS.   (280)

When economy has to be considered, quite an attractive accompaniment to fried bacon or sausage can be made as follows :—

Cut fingers of Vienna bread about ⅜ of an inch thick, soak in milk for a few minutes, then dip in beaten egg, well seasoned with salt and pepper. Fry quickly in smoking bacon fat, drain well and dish in a border, faggot fashion, round the bacon.

ANCHOVY SANDWICH PASTE.   (281)

4 Eggs.	2 tablespoonsful Anchovy Essence.
4 ozs. Butter.	Pinches of Nutmeg and Mace.

Boil the eggs for 20 minutes and put in cold water. When cold remove the yolks and pound in a mortar with the butter, anchovy essence and seasonings. When perfectly blended put into pots and run clarified butter over the top.

HONEY AND OATMEAL SANDWICHES. (282)

One of the chief drawbacks to honey as a filling for sandwiches is its thinness, which is apt to make them sticky to touch and unpleasant to look upon. This can be overcome in a way which is in itself a great improvement to the usual bread and honey. Take two handfuls of oatmeal and put it in the oven till it turns a pale brown and lay aside to cool. Spread brown bread with fresh butter or margarine and cut in thin slices. Spread alternate slices with honey from the comb and sprinkle with the toasted oatmeal. Cover with bread and butter and press. Just before serving trim off the crusts and cut into fingers. These sandwiches are best made only a short time before they are eaten. When the oatmeal is sufficiently brown it will have a pleasant nutty flavour.

RED CURRANT JELLY SANDWICHES. (283)

. Cut five slices of very thin white bread and butter.
Spread four of them with red currant jelly and lay the
fifth on top. Press between two boards. With a very
sharp knife cut crosswise into fingers and arrange them
faggot fashion rejecting, of course, the crusts on either side.

WALNUT SANDWICH FILLING. (284)

According to the quantity required whip up cream till
it just hangs from the whisk, add sufficient finely chopped
salted walnuts to make a fairly soft paste. Spread
between thin slices of brown bread and butter. Press
between two plates till wanted, then trim off the crusts
with a very sharp knife. Cut into shapes and garnish
with cress. It is not necessary to butter the bread.

TO FOLD IN WHITE OF EGG. (285)

Many recipes require that the whites of eggs shall be
" folded in," and few, if any, tell one how this is to be
accomplished. It is surprising how many persons ask for
more explicit directions. Cakes, puddings and soufflés to
which very stiffly beaten whites of eggs are added are, as
a rule, mixed with a wooden spoon. When it comes to
the time for adding the whites, remove this spoon and
substitute a plated or metal one. Add the whites and
turn the mixture over with a plated spoon. Cut through
it, lift it up and fold the materials together going well
down to the bottom of the basin and gently continuing
this folding over of the mixture till just blended. Do not
stir round and round, or beat, after folding in the eggs.

TO SHRED SUET.   (286)

If suet is carefully prepared suet puddings are much lighter and the possibility of meeting pieces of unmelted suet in the pudding is very remote.

To prepare it take a firm piece of fresh beef suet and remove the skin. With a sharp knife shred it very finely so that it curls up and the particles resemble Lux in their thinness. After this has been done and the required quantity weighed or measured it may be chopped with some of the flour for the pudding dredged amongst it. The flour keeps all the particles free and dry.

TO SWEAT VEGETABLES.   (287)

This means to cook them over heat in fat till they have absorbed it all.   When this has been done there should be no grease on the top of the soup.

SEPARATING EGGS.   (288)

In separating yolks from whites, if the shell is very brittle the operation is not always a complete success.   To remove any yolk which gets into the white, dip a clean cloth in hot water and just touch the yolk, which will adhere to it.

COOK BOOK COVER.   (289)

Many people complain of the stained and splashed condition of their treasured cookery books after they have been in use in the kitchen for some time.   With the best intentions in the world these accidents do happen, but one can at least take steps to prevent them.

The most simple method is to use a sheet of glass rather larger than the open book. The glass is delightful to use if it is bevelled, but a simple passe-partout, or even stamp paper, binding answers very well indeed. This serves the double purpose of keeping the book clean and the page flat out.

GARDENING HINT. (290)

Before going to the garden, scratch a piece of fairly soft soap till the space between the nail and the finger is quite filled up. Then apply a layer round the base of the nail. This will dry quickly and prevent the soil from getting in, and has the advantage of being easily removed with a nail brush.

TO WASH HAIR BRUSHES. (291)

Put 1 teaspoonful Sophos into a shallow basin and fill up with hot water. Dip the bristles in this till clean. Rinse in cold water and dry in a draught.

TO WASH AND DRESS A SHETLAND SHAWL. (292)

The finishing of a Shetland shawl is very simple when one knows how to set about it.

The shawl should be washed in warm water and Lux to which has been added a few drops of Petrel ammonia.

Do not rub the shawl nor wring it but work it gently between the hands till clean. Squeeze out as much water as possible and wash in the same way in a second soapy water. Squeeze out as much of the soapy water as possible and rinse in slightly blued water, keeping all three waters of the same temperature.

Fold the shawl in a towel and pass through a wringer and shake very well.

· Have ready a good strong barrel and in the bottom of it have an iron dish with a piece of rock sulphur broken up in it.   Pour over the sulphur a few drops of methylated spirits and light it.

Take two sticks long enough to lie across the barrel and over these fold the shawl.   When the flame from the spirits has gone down lay the sticks across the barrel and cover with an old blanket to keep in the fumes.

Leave it exposed to the fumes for $\frac{3}{4}$ of an hour, turning it from time to time so that each part is done.

After bleaching in this way, thread four pieces of fine string through the points of the shawl and lay it out on a stretched sheet to dry, pulling the strings tight and fixing them with push pins so that the edges are perfectly even. When quite dry iron lightly over with a cool iron and fold.

HOLEPROOF STOCKINGS.   (293)
(Excellent).

When the stockings are new turn them outside in and apply a small piece of cambric or fine calico about $2\frac{1}{2} \times 2$ inches over the part of the heel where the most wear comes.   Measure where the edge of the shoe comes, and see that the patch is well above it.   Hem this on with a fine cotton or silk the exact shade of the stockings, but do not put a lay on the calico.   Sew a semi-circular piece on the toe.   If this is carefully done, it will be found perfectly comfortable and almost invisible on the outside. One may have to renew the patches when no hole has appeared on the stocking, so examine them from day to day.

The Westburn Sugar Refineries Ltd.

Greenock

Why use "WESTBURN" *Golden Syrup?*

BECAUSE
> Of its wonderful purity and rich quality.

BECAUSE
> Money cannot buy anything better.

BECAUSE
> "WESTBURN" is a home-produced article, and you are helping to employ local labour.

BECAUSE
> "WESTBURN" is an article that should be in every household.

BAKING POWDER

N O HOME SHOULD BE WITHOUT THIS
WORLD-RENOWNED PREPARATION,
WHICH MAKES **BREAD, CAKES,**
PASTRY, etc., LIGHT AND DIGESTIBLE.

A Good Plain Cake

Mix well together 1 lb. of Flour, 2 large teaspoonsfuls of
Borwick's Baking Powder, a little Salt and Spice, and ¼ lb. of
Sugar, rub in 6 ozs. Margarine, add 6 ozs. of Sultanas, 2 ozs. of
Currants, and 1 oz. of Candied Peel. Moisten the whole with 1 Egg
and 1 teacupful of Milk previously beaten together. Bake in a
quick oven for about 1¼ hours.

Scotch Drop Scones

8 ozs. Flour.
1½ teaspoonsful **Borwick's Baking Powder.**
2 ozs. Margarine.
1 tablespoonful Golden Syrup.
Pinch of Salt.
A little Milk.

Sieve flour, baking powder, and salt into a basin, rub in the
margarine with the tips of fingers, add the golden syrup and
sufficient milk to make a light dough. Drop in small heaps on a
Scotch gridiron, place on the top of the stove, and cook on each side.

Plain Raisin Pudding

Take 1 lb. of Flour and mix with it 2 teaspoonsful of **Borwick's
Baking Powder,** ½ lb. of Stoned Raisins, 2 teaspoonsful of
Demerara Sugar. Mix with enough water to form a moist pudding,
put into a greased basin, tie in a cloth, and boil for 2 hours.

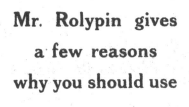

ECONOMY IN YOUR KITCHEN MUST APPEAL TO YOU

MARMITE

IS THE EXTRACT YOU SHOULD USE FOR
MAKING AND ENRICHING ALL

Soups, Sauces, Stews Gravies, Sandwiches, etc.

Note these Points.

1.—MARMITE is low in price.

2.—MARMITE is most economical in use.

3.—MARMITE, owing to its richness in vitamines, is good for you and your children.

4.—MARMITE increases vitality and thus staves off influenza and chills.

5.—MARMITE keeps the strong fit and builds up the weakly.

6.—MARMITE taken last thing at night induces refreshing sleep.

Note these Prices.

1 oz. jar **6**d.	4 oz. jar **1/6**
2 oz. jar **10**d.	8 oz. jar **2/6**
16 oz. jar **4/6**	

L